TIMELESS

ORO EDITIONS

Publishers of Architecture, Art, and Design

Gordon Goff: Publisher

www.oroeditions.com
info@oroeditions.com

Published by ORO EDITIONS INC.

TEXT BY
Patrick Ahearn

WRITTEN WITH
Andrew Sessa

P.A. ARCHITECT MARKETING DIRECTOR
Katherine Nolan

ORO EDITIONS MANAGING EDITOR
Jake Anderson

BOOK DESIGNER
Pablo Mandel / CircularStudio.com

Typeset in Rieux and Minion Pro

10 9 8 7 6 5 4 3

Library of Congress data available upon request.

ISBN: 978-1-939621-93-1

Color Separations and Printing: ORO GROUP LTD.
Printed in China.

International Distribution: www.oroeditions.com/distribution

ORO EDITIONS makes a continuous effort to minimize the overall carbon footprint of its publications.
As part of this goal, ORO EDITIONS, in association with Global ReLeaf, arranges to plant trees to replace
those used in the manufacturing of the paper produced for its books. Global ReLeaf is an international
campaign run by American Forests, one of the world's oldest nonprofit conservation organizations.
Global ReLeaf is American Forests' education and action program that helps individuals, organizations,
agencies, and corporations improve the local and global environment by planting and caring for trees.

TIMELESS

CLASSIC AMERICAN ARCHITECTURE
FOR CONTEMPORARY LIVING

PATRICK AHEARN

CONTENTS

DEDICATION

This book is for Howard Elkus, a mentor,
colleague, and friend without whom
my career would have been very different.

My relationship with Howard began back in the mid-1970s. I was barely out of school, working as an architect and urban designer at The Architects Collaborative — the pioneering modernist firm started by Bauhaus founder Walter Gropius in Cambridge, Massachusetts — where Howard was then an associate. We hadn't yet worked together, but after he heard about a certain large-scale, complex model I'd made for some of the firm's partners, he sought out my help on a project. Together, we started working after hours, swapping sketches and honing the concept for a new tower at Boston University.

That particular project never came to fruition, but from this collaboration, and from other opportunities I had to see Howard at work in the years that followed, I learned a tremendous amount. Through Howard, I discovered how to create sensitive, historically appropriate designs that preserve and respect their urban contexts while innovatively enriching their communities and improving contemporary lives. Beyond design, Howard also taught me how to convey a vision and captivate an audience. He was as much a showman as an architect, and there simply was no one better than him at selling an idea.

Working with Howard gave me the skills, the confidence, and the knowledge I needed to strike out and start my own firm. When I eventually did so, I began by taking on the same sort of adaptive-reuse projects as those at which he excelled, albeit on a much smaller scale, at least initially.

Long after we stopped working together, I ran into Howard in the restaurant of a private club I'd designed in the village of Edgartown, on Martha's Vineyard. Even three decades later, he was the same old Howard, taking over the room, holding court, and keeping everyone's rapt attention as he told story after story of our shared adventure in architecture.

When Howard passed away suddenly in April 2017, at the age of seventy-eight, he was more than fifty years into his career and still hard at work. He was a mentor to and a model for me, and I miss him greatly.

Among the buildings that define his impressive legacy is the headquarters of the American Institute of Architects, in Washington, D.C. — an organization that subsequently made him one of its youngest Fellows ever. Howard would later go on to write the letter of nomination that led to my own elevation to Fellow of the American Institute of Architects, a favor and an honor for which I will be forever grateful.

After he died, his architect daughter, Jenny Elkus, told the Boston Globe that Howard didn't think of himself as having employees, and he didn't think of himself as having clients; he felt he had only friends. I consider myself lucky to have been among them.

FOREWORD

*It had long been my intention to have the foreword of this book written by
the eminent Boston architect Howard Elkus. Howard died quite suddenly
in the spring of 2017, and so, in his honor and memory, I instead share the
introductory letter he wrote in support of my elevation to a Fellow of the
American Institute of Architects in 2014.*

ELKUS | MANFREDI
ARCHITECTS

September 29, 2014

Sponsor's Letter of Recommendation for Patrick Ahearn's Election to Fellowship in the AIA

It is a great honor and privilege to have been asked to sponsor Patrick Ahearn for Fellowship in the
American Institute of Architects. His career has been emblematic of the unique opportunity and
responsibility of our profession to preserve, sustain, and contribute to the future of our great
architectural heritage. His legacy is deservedly assured through his truly remarkable personal and
professional commitment to the island of Martha's Vineyard and most specifically to the community
of Edgartown. It is a story that parallels that of the legendary Addison Mizner in the Palm Beaches,
both as a gifted designer and as an entrepreneur, and beyond that a purposeful benefactor.

I have known Patrick since we had the pleasure of working together at The Architects Collaborative in
the 1970's. Since that time, Patrick has established an impressive reputation through his work in
Boston's historic Back Bay residential neighborhood where he has been a major force as a pioneer in
its preservation and revitalization through the extent and quality of his own work, both as an architect
and as the Boston Society of Architects' representative on the Back Bay Architectural Commission.

Beyond his meritable contribution to Boston, it is the impact he has had in Edgartown through his
investment of time, energy, and talent which I think really sets Patrick apart. He has totally captured
and preserved the essence of scale, character, materiality, and richness of detail which distinguishes
this historic seaside village in the homes and civic structures he has so creatively designed and
restored regardless of size or use. The staggering aggregation of properties and public spaces his
hand has touched also attest to his prowess as a gifted urban designer.

All of this has been recognized in an exceptional accumulation of design awards and publications
throughout his career culminating in his recent induction into the New England Design Hall of Fame.
What I think is equally worth citing is his outstanding contribution as leader, teacher, and benefactor
helping to guide, educate, and enable a democratic society to value, preserve, and enhance the built
environment. Whether it be in public gatherings, in the media, or as an alumnus of the Syracuse
University School of Architecture, he is "out there" commanding respect for the architectural
profession.

Howard F Elkus FAIA, RIBA, LEED AP
Co-Founder

INTRODUCTION

Throughout my forty-five-year career, two core beliefs have inspired me and shaped my architecture: that design — good design — has the power to improve people's lives and that learning from the past is crucial to creating the future. Together, these principles have led me to craft timeless, human-scaled private homes and public environments that balance preservation with innovation. Sitting lightly on the land and seamlessly integrated into their streetscapes and broader context, these authentically classical buildings, whether historic or historically motivated, not only accommodate, but also enhance how we live today.

Beyond their enduring aesthetic, the spaces my firm designs increase their occupants' well-being, encourage friendly interactions, and help build a sense of community. We make architecture for the greater good — not for the aggrandizement of our clients or ourselves but to strengthen the urban and social fabric into which it is woven. The buildings we create are the better for it, improving the lives of those who occupy, and interact with, them.

In these pages, I will explain how I adapted and applied the idea of philosophy's greater-good theory to my architectural pursuits, and then describe how I turn these into engaging environments that honor the past, enrich the present, and look toward the future. With this book, I hope to inspire others — both architects and homeowners — to build better, smarter, and for the benefit of their communities.

Driven by Design

By the time I was four or five, I knew I wanted to be a designer. But I didn't think I was going to devote my career to architecture. Instead, I wanted to design cars.

I have my father to thank for my automotive obsession, a fascination that continues to this day. Dad was a car guy, buying a new one every few years: a moss green 1949 Studebaker, a white 1953 Ford Victoria with a navy hardtop, a red-and-white 1955 Ford Country Sedan station wagon, a turquoise 1957 Mercury Villager hardtop station wagon, an aquamarine 1960 Ford Galaxie Town Victoria, a red 1962 Pontiac Catalina convertible, to name a few.

I still remember riding to the local bakery every weekend in that '53 Ford, with its curvaceous white-and-blue exterior and matching two-tone interior. I can picture the simple face and numerals of the round chrome bezel clock in the middle of the metal dash, feel the smooth texture of the seat's woven fabric beneath me. These sensations are embedded not just in my memory, but in my psyche as well.

I used to savor the opportunity to wash Dad's cars, to experience them with my hands. Doing so let me feel the sculptural lines and learn even more about the shape and form than I could by looking. As I washed those cars, I came to love them as design objects.

Eventually, I started sending away for brochures for more exotic autos. I'd buy vellum at the art-supply store and trace the lines of the vehicles again and again. Through these early experiences, I came to understand the importance of scale, proportion, and light, and to appreciate that quality design could make you feel something special.

The Lessons of Levittown

If cars sparked my earliest aesthetic awareness, growing up in the suburbs of New York City awakened me to the importance of architecture and urban design, and their ability to foster a sense of community. This was because I didn't grow up in just any suburb; I grew up in Levittown. Laid out in the late 1940s and early '50s on former Long Island potato fields by developer William Levitt and his architect brother, Alfred, Levittown is to the suburb what the Model T is to the car: a pioneer of mass-produced good design that changed society.

The Levitts built their town as the nation's first planned suburb, its 17,447 nearly identical Cape Cod– and ranch-style houses created

NO. 1

NO. 2

REAR VIEW OF ALL HOUSES

THE

1950 House of Levittown

•

**TELEVISION EQUIPPED
by ADMIRAL!**

•

Complete Price - $7990

NO. 3

NO. 4

ABOVE: Although the floor plans and rear elevations of all Levittown houses were the same, the community's developers offered potential homeowners four different front façades. My family lived in the No. 1 model.

for GIS returning from war. They each measured 832 square feet and had identical two-bedroom floor plans, with only slight variations in their façades and how they sat on their plots of land. A finished house, complete with crabapple and willow trees, could be yours for $7,990 — or $100 down and $66 a month.

Levittown taught me vital lessons and principles that I've carried through my career. It made me appreciate density and scale, and the balance between the two: the community was spread out over just a few square miles, but the homes' modest size turned their concentration into a virtue. The Levitts understood that the space between buildings was just as important as the houses themselves, because it helped mitigate any sense of claustrophobia. Strips of grass flanked sidewalks, and weeping willows separated houses. This let light and air flow through and lent a sense of timelessness to the streetscape of Levittown's newly constructed 1,001 curving lanes.

Density also allowed for easy walkability, which was further fostered by smart circulation and connectivity. Fences were prohibited, letting my friends and me run from yard to yard, block to block, while pedestrian paths enabled us to ride our bikes or walk from our front doors to Levittown's many parks, ball fields, village greens, schools, and swimming pools.

Levittown's houses were spare, but they evoked warm feelings of hearth and home nonetheless. We welcomed little luxuries like two-sided fireplaces, radiant floor heating, and built-in televisions, plus floor plans that created gathering points where our family could convene and celebrate. Large, double-height windows on the back of every house filled the space with natural light, linking indoors and out, further connecting us to our neighbors.

The floor plans were easily adjustable, thanks to the smart inclusions of swiveling cabinets and room dividers, and they were designed to expand — one neighbor after another added bedrooms upstairs. This adaptability proved to be one of the secrets of Levittown's longevity, letting successive generations of homeowners reimagine and customize the buildings.

I absorbed all this as I grew up — before I was ten, I was making little models of the local houses for my American Flyer train set. The lessons of Levittown led me to architecture, and that, eventually, brought me to New England.

For the Love of Boston

After earning degrees in architecture and urban design from Syracuse University, where my education focused on modernism, I made my way to Maine to begin the next stage of my life with a sailing trip down the Atlantic Coast. This was my first real experience of New England, and I found myself entirely enamored. Of all the charming little towns I visited, it was Marblehead, Massachusetts, that most opened my eyes to the romance and ingenuity of the region's architecture. In this historic seaside village — whose brightly painted, gable-roofed clapboard houses sit cheek-by-jowl — I saw the same sensitivity to density, scale, and walkability I so admired in Levittown. But here, all was rendered in the inviting and unmistakably local Colonial vernacular of its original construction.

Soon after leaving that port, I sailed into Boston Harbor. Walking around the city, I saw the architecture and urban design of Marblehead

writ large across Boston's streets and neighborhoods. I came to realize that density on this scale could create an incredibly rich way of life, one that suggested an appealing alternative to both my suburban upbringing and a modern metropolis like Manhattan. People resided and worked in centuries-old spaces above and below boutiques and little restaurants, down hidden alleys and narrow streets. It felt like living history — as if past and present intertwined — and I wanted to be a part of it.

Within weeks of arriving in Boston, I'd found myself a basement apartment in the Back Bay and a job at a small firm. I hopped from one bigger and better firm to the next through the early 1970s, teaching nights at Boston Architectural College, and eventually landed at Benjamin Thompson & Associates. There, my work on the revitalization of Boston's historic Faneuil Hall area introduced me to the power of adaptive reuse projects and narrative-driven architecture to build a sense of community.

By reinventing a series of empty eighteenth- and nineteenth-century buildings and turning the spaces between them into public plazas, we created the first so-called "festival marketplace" in the country. We began by scripting a new program that would transform the abandoned district into a vibrant, multiuse public environment, imagining the tables of a seafood restaurant here, a flower vendor selling blooms from a pushcart there, street performers dotting the periphery, and huge garage doors to connect indoors to out. This retail, dining, entertainment, and cultural hub has become Boston's most-visited site, today attracting some eighteen million people a year. Faneuil Hall Marketplace made me appreciate how creating an architectural storyline can elevate people's enjoyment and understanding of a reimagined space.

From the Back Bay to Martha's Vineyard

While teaching and working for various Boston firms, I also began redesigning historic townhouses in the then-struggling Back Bay. Collaborating with developers, I restored the buildings' grand, landmark-protected nineteenth-century façades, then remade their long-neglected interiors as clean-lined, open-plan spaces with Charles River–facing rear walls of glass — a lesson from Levittown — that opened to new terraces. Ever mindful of the scale, proportions, and context of the neighborhood, I became a darling of zoning regulators, conservation committees, and community boards, able to find appropriate but novel architectural solutions that pleased both preservationists and innovators. I quickly became the go-to guy for these contemporary interventions and eventually started buying and renovating properties myself.

Based on the success of these projects, I launched my own firm, taking studio space back in Faneuil Hall Marketplace. This proved especially apt, as I leveraged what I'd learned there to reinvigorate Newbury Street. As at Faneuil, I scripted a new narrative for this avenue, the Back Bay's main commercial corridor. There would be cafés with outdoor seating, boutiques with welcoming window displays, widened sidewalks, and narrowed roadways. The scheme looked to the main streets of decades past even as it created a new contemporary reality, and, like Faneuil, it proved a big hit.

By the late 1980s, I'd renovated hundreds of historic Back Bay buildings, taking the neighborhood from dilapidated to desirable. While contemplating my next venture, I was introduced to a woman at a client's birthday party on Beacon Hill. That meeting proved auspicious: not only did Marsha become my wife, we rediscovered Edgartown together, the postcard-perfect, centuries-old community on Martha's Vineyard to which I've devoted most of my professional and personal energies ever since.

When Marsha and I first started going to Edgartown we immediately fell for its small-town feel. It felt sublimely intimate in scale, densely compact, and highly walkable, just like Marblehead and the Levittown of my youth. And then there was the aesthetic: white picket fences between brick sidewalks and shallow green lawns, behind which sat shingled and clapboard, traditional and neoclassical bungalows and cottages, with whaling captains' homes along the harbor's edge.

Despite being charmed by Edgartown, I didn't view the village as a place to take on work, seeing it more as an inspiring location to rest and recharge. I began to recognize the opportunities to restore many of its homes and to reinvigorate and improve the street life in its waterfront downtown core, but I was still very much focused on the Back Bay. Even after we bought and renovated our first Edgartown house, a simple colonial replica, I didn't start a single project on the Vineyard for quite some time. Then, one summer five years later, I decided to test the waters by placing a recurring ad in the local newspaper, each time featuring a sketch for a different "house of the week." Lo and behold, by the end of the season, I had twenty-six commissions.

In the three decades since, I've completed more than 200 projects on Martha's Vineyard, 160 of them in Edgartown Village alone. Beyond the residences, my public and commercial work includes the reinvention of the 1960s harbor-side former Navigator Building as the Atlantic restaurant and Boathouse club, a dining, entertainment, and retail venue that brought new life to Main Street and provided public access to the waterfront.

My revitalization of Edgartown has been the most rewarding project of my career and the epitome of the greater-good theory put into practice. The homes and environments I've created there have shown that preservation properly balanced with innovation can create timeless architecture that improves the way we live, work, and play, both as individuals and as a community.

An Architectural Journey

This book offers an exclusive tour of many of my Edgartown projects, as well as homes I've designed throughout New England — the birthplace of vernacular American architectural styles from Colonial to Georgian, Federal to Greek Revival to Victorian.

Chapter One looks at how I've *preserved* landmarked residences to restore them to their original beauty, and Chapter Two examines the *enhancement* of centuries-old houses ravaged by age and unsympathetic renovations. Chapter Three focuses on how *modernized* interiors can take shape within historic walls, while Chapters Four and Five involve newly built dwellings — the former, ones that *imagine* designs that are all but indistinguishable from historic dwellings, and the latter those that *reinterpret* local vernacular architecture in especially novel ways. Chapter Six pays special attention to the challenges and rewards of designing and building on the *waterfront*, and the Afterword draws important lessons and insights from place-making *public works* like Faneuil Hall

Marketplace and the Atlantic/Boathouse building in Edgartown.

The projects collected in these pages combine the romance and nostalgia of traditional architecture with the ideas and ideals of modernism. Their designs balance preservation with innovation in classical buildings that look and feel like they have stood the test of time, even if they are only a few years old.

I hope you will enjoy discovering my work as much as I enjoyed creating it and that the lessons I've learned about the transformative power of timeless good design will inspire and enlighten you.

PATRICK AHEARN ARCHITECT
Boston · 617.266.1710 · Edgartown

ABOVE: My work in Edgartown, on Martha's Vineyard, began in the summer of 1994 with the "house of the week" sketches I placed in the *Vineyard Gazette* newspaper every Friday.

OPPOSITE: Inspired by automotive design and local agrarian architecture, my Edgartown "Car Barn" displays my classic car collection downstairs with living space above.

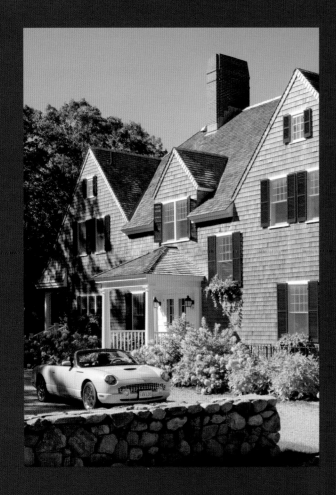
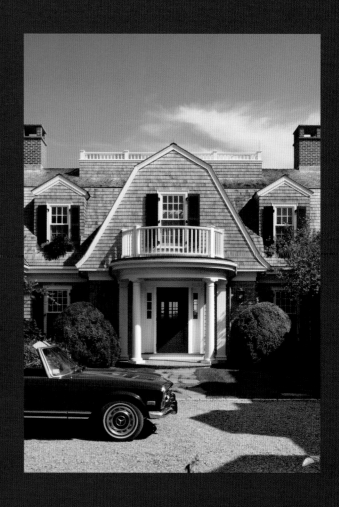

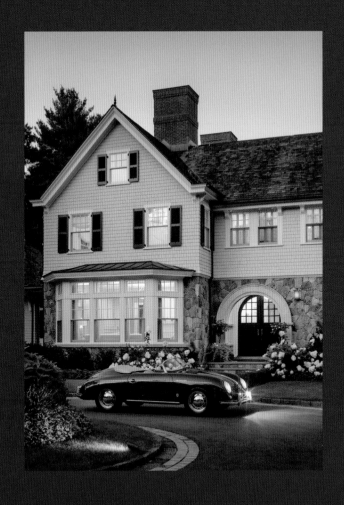

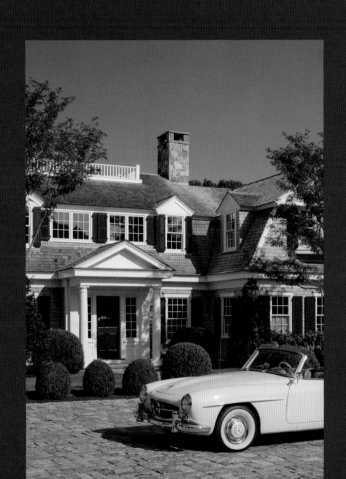
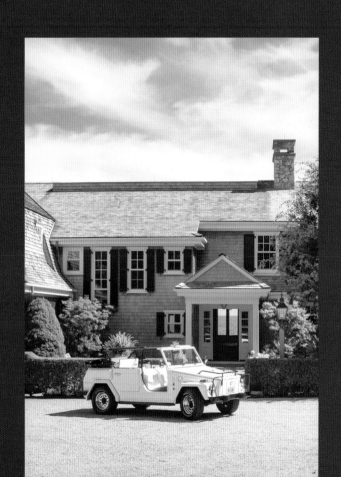

1

History Preserved

The goal of non-ego-driven architecture is for the designer to slip entirely from view. Only then can timeless buildings fully contribute to the greater good of their occupants and their broader communities. I often say, in fact, that if I have done my job correctly, I will be like a ghost who visits in the night — leaving no trace and most successful when no one sees my hand.

This philosophy is especially vital when working on the type of project presented in this chapter: houses that are protected as landmarks, with impeccable provenance and historical significance. This is architecture for the greater good in the most fundamental sense: it enriches villages and cities by preserving iconic structures essential to our collective memory. These buildings make old places matter, lending communities character and context, providing precedents for other structures, and enhancing the human experience in architecturally important places like Boston's Back Bay and the village of Edgartown on Martha's Vineyard. When renovating them, I am particularly aware of my responsibility to sustain, celebrate, and contribute to the aesthetic heritage of America.

In every commission I take on, I see it as my duty to balance preservation with innovation, but in the case of the houses collected in this chapter, the scales tip decidedly toward the former. While not quite museums, the resulting structure are certainly intended to be museum-like, so creating them requires me to work as an archaeologist, historian, curator, and conservator all at once. My watchwords are research, restoration, and, ultimately, rebirth.

These projects are not devoid of innovation, however. Preservation demands feats of engineering and design ingenuity. And because the restored residences are meant to be truly lived in by their current occupants and successive generations, they must be brought up to date, no matter how much conservation work we do or how many antiques fill them when we're done.

This is where the architect comes in as the ghost in the night. The trick is to seamlessly, imperceptibly introduce updates rooted in the real history of the home. A building's broader context always guides my work, but with these preservation projects, the house's extant architecture provides the most important contextual clues.

Renovation and expansion of landmarks must proceed with a heightened sensitivity to and awareness of the homes' existing architectural elements, scale, and proportions, as well as those of the surrounding landscape. Architects must strive to honor these inherent characteristics both as they preserve and as they innovate. The details matter here — the pitch of a roof, the weight of a door latch, the patina of the brick — because in the end, they are what provide authenticity.

Often, preservation as prescribed by a local landmarks board seems to conflict with a client's desired program. Finding appropriate solutions requires great design skill, creative problem solving, profound respect for the integrity of the home's past, and a wide-ranging knowledge of classical American architecture. Pleasing all sides also demands a deep understanding of zoning regulations and the mandates of local historic commissions, plus strong persuasive abilities to make your case before the necessary commissions. You must learn to serve as both professor and community activist, a vital combination when educating a client about the importance of history and context. The patience of a saint helps, too.

Preserving the three Edgartown landmarks presented here — all of them on the village's prominent South Water Street — was not without challenges. The hard thinking required by these complications improved the final outcome, however, and today the rewards that the restored homes provide both to their occupants and to the larger village community are manifold.

OPPOSITE: Working on landmarked houses — like Edgartown's Ellis Lewis House, where I restored and expanded the Federal-style mid-1800s building — demands that painstaking preservation initiatives, and any renovations and additions, remain all but invisible.

ABOVE AND RIGHT: The Thomas Cooke House II, a 1790 Edgartown Colonial, features a new pool and cabana, plus rear and carriage house wings — none of it visible from the street.

PATRICK AHEARN

ABOVE, TOP: In Chatham, on Cape Cod, I restored the circa-1826 Wheelwright House, guest cottage, and carriage house and added a new pool and landscaping.

ABOVE, BOTTOM: Impeccably preserved, Edgartown's 1840 Greek Revival Captain Thomas Adams Norton House seamlessly integrates a new secondary entrance, dormers, and an attached carriage house.

OPPOSITE: Era-appropriate details matter — I used such carefully chosen exterior components as antique bricks, slate roofing, and copper fascia and flashing when restoring this home in Wellesley, Massachusetts, just outside of Boston.

A BLACKSMITH'S HOME REBORN

**Edgartown Village Historic District,
Martha's Vineyard, Massachusetts**

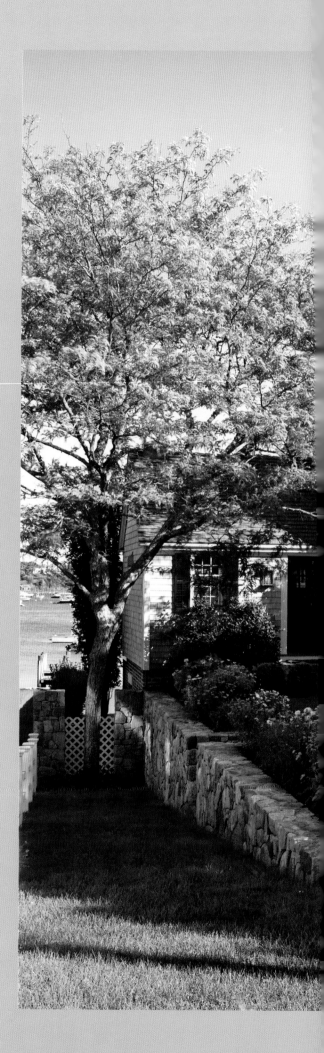

WHEN BLACKSMITH JOHN COFFIN built his shed-roof residence and shop on Edgartown's harbor, in 1682, could he ever have imagined that a modern family would call it home today? Since its construction, the Colonial-style structure, today known as the John Coffin House, has lived many lives. Expanded through several additions, some better, some worse, it has housed a succession of craftsmen and been subjected to significant wear and tear.

RIGHT: Built in 1682 by the first blacksmith on Martha's Vineyard, the John Coffin House is one of Edgartown's most historic residences. Today, it welcomes its twenty-first-century owners as a flawlessly preserved and sensitively expanded multigenerational summer compound.

LEFT: Archival research uncovered circa-1890 images of the house, which we used as a guide for our work on the property.

OPPOSITE: Although larger than the original, the new enclosed front portico remains true to its centuries-old antecedent.

In 2005, when we were commissioned, the original twenty-four-by-thirty-two-foot dwelling was severely unstable. The new owners wanted to restore its glory, and they also needed to expand its program to accommodate their multigenerational family. We developed a restoration plan and designed additional spaces in several historically motivated outbuildings that now serve as a guest cottage, carriage house, and home office. Their exteriors take inspiration from 1890s additions discovered in archival research. The structures sit naturally in the existing topography, preserving the public's view of the water and suggesting that the seaside compound developed over time — a narrative typical of traditional New England architecture and one that I return to again and again.

The outbuildings' interiors, meanwhile, encourage twenty-first-century living. A new lower level in the original house does the same, containing a media room, a game room, a wine cellar, and a tavern with a fireplace that replicates John Coffin's blacksmithing furnace. Created thanks to a new foundation — which, together with the surgical replacement of each post and beam, stabilized the building — this garden level opens to a bluestone patio, a lawn, and the harbor beyond.

In the main house, we restored most interiors and re-created others using existing materials: more than 80 percent of the wood in the building is from 1682. Rooms remained in their original locations, the seventeenth-century-scaled spaces virtually unchanged, albeit meticulously preserved. New framing supports original wide-plank floors, and a restored 1682 bay window illuminates the foyer, which is warmed by a refurbished Rumford-style fireplace original to the house.

Now, the character not just of the 1682 building but of the entire compound celebrates its age, scale, and historic import, while fostering the easy living and entertaining we value today.

OPPOSITE: Over 80 percent of the wood used in the renovation — including the beams in the new master study — date back to the house's 1682 roots.

ABOVE AND RIGHT: Based on a historic image of the home's harbor-facing elevation, we decided to place a breakfast room and sunroom within what looks like an enclosed former porch.

PATRICK AHEARN

WHALING'S GOLDEN ERA

**Edgartown Village Historic District,
Martha's Vineyard, Massachusetts**

THE RICH HISTORY of Edgartown's Captain Rufus Pease House — also known as the Yellow House because of the distinctive hue of its clapboard cladding — has captivated Vineyard locals and visitors for decades. Built in 1838, when the whaling industry was at its peak, the impressive Georgian Colonial was home to Captain Rufus F. Pease for more than fifty years, from 1840 to 1893, including his time as the island's commissioner of wrecks and shipwrecked goods. By the time our work on the building started, in 2015, it was something of a wreck itself. Our mission was to erase the damage done by years of severe weather, benign neglect, and anachronistic additions, while dramatically improving the interior's flow and water views.

RIGHT: Following the restoration of the Captain Rufus Pease House, built in Edgartown in 1838, nearly every element of its construction is new — and historically correct.

When we finished, nearly every element of the house's exterior and
structure was new. This included everything from the foundation and the
brick veneer covering it to the posts, beams, and roof, as well as all the
heating, cooling, plumbing, and electrical systems. But because of our
ability to operate like that ghost in the night, the building looks just as it
did in the 1840s.

By working within the existing footprint and replacing a mid-
twentieth-century rear addition with one sympathetic to the original
architecture, we allowed the Yellow House to be truer to itself and its
history than it had been for fifty years. Inside, with minimal intervention
but maximum innovation, we reoriented the structure to simplify
circulation and take advantage of rear-facing water views. A central spine
— a hallmark of modern interiors that I frequently deploy in older homes
without detracting from their history — now connects the rooms from
front to back, establishing long views through the building. A restored
main staircase extends to the new basement, with exact replicas of the
1838 newel posts and balustrades. Throughout, we reclaimed, refinished,
and reinstalled materials and re-created designs for the wood-plank
flooring, hardware, and mill-, brick-, and stonework that had been
original to the house, ensuring its seamlessness.

Even as it remains entirely faithful to its origins, the Captain Rufus
Pease House today projects a newfound vitality, ready to serve as a living
heirloom for generations to come.

OPPOSITE: The entry — with its 1838 floors and balustrade, which now continues into a new lower level — immediately transports visitors back in time.

RIGHT: Occupying the building's former study, the home office features new built-ins designed to match existing early-nineteenth-century window moldings.

ABOVE: I preserved the tiny door — now in the middle of the blue backsplash tile —connecting the kitchen to the mudroom. Historically, the cook would have used it to see who was arriving at the home's service entrance.

OPPOSITE: Open to the kitchen, the dining room sits in a new addition whose period-appropriate windows and antique flooring match those in the restored portion of the house.

CORRECTING
THE HISTORICAL
RECORD

Edgartown Village Historic District,
Martha's Vineyard, Massachusetts

DESPITE HOLDING PRIDE of place in
Edgartown's historic district, this clapboard-
fronted Federal Colonial–style former captain's
home, originally constructed at some point
between 1886 and 1898, was in significant
disrepair. Most of the original interior and
exterior detail had been removed or modified
beyond recognition, and only the basic
massing of the two-and-a-half-story hip-roofed
clapboard- and shingle-clad structure remained.
Without access to the on-site contextual clues
that usually lead our preservation projects, we
turned to the archival record.

RIGHT: Before its preservation, only the basic
massing of this former captain's home in
Edgartown remained intact. I found photos
documenting the clapboard-fronted Federal
Colonial's late-nineteenth-century origins, which
led to the visual language of its restoration and
carriage house extension.

At the local museum, we found late-nineteenth-century photographs of the house and used these to build the visual language for the project. We then began the restoration in earnest, once again placing the home on an updated foundation. This created a new lower level containing a family room, guest room and bath, master suite, and service entry with mudroom and laundry, all of it invisible from the street but, thanks to a grade change in the landscape, open to the harbor at the rear. The archival images suggested that a water-facing porch once existed upstairs, and we leveraged that information to create an enclosed sunroom with sweeping port views just off the kitchen, finishing it with full-height beadboard walls, baseboards, and crown moldings, plus antique brick floors and timber ceiling beams from the 1800s.

Not only is this house a prime example of sensitive preservation, but it's also a particularly strong model of the greater-good theory. The restoration of its façade, as well as the development of its front yard, dramatically improve the overall streetscape. The home now lives up to the promise of its central location on South Water Street, unifying and enhancing the Historic District's harbor front and increasing the enjoyment of anyone who walks past.

RIGHT: In the beadboard-paneled kitchen, turned-leg details give custom cabinetry the look of furniture. French doors open to a balcony with views to the pool and dock.

FOLLOWING PAGES: Encouraging easy indoor-outdoor living, the casual family room leads onto a dining terrace, then down to the lawn, pool, and water.

ABOVE: The new garden-level master suite enjoys access to a private terrace through the bay window's French doors.

OPPOSITE: The soaking tub in the master bath sits in a windowed alcove with enviable views of Edgartown Harbor.

FOLLOWING PAGES: The expanded house revels in its waterfront position with three-and-a-half stories of glazing and ample opportunities for alfresco entertaining.

2

History Enhanced

While the centuries-old homes in the previous chapter rarely compelled me to look beyond their own walls or rich pasts for authentic inspiration and motivation, the younger residences in this section sometimes required me to dig deeper to find a history to build on. Old houses don't all have the intrinsic historical significance of a landmark nor the same obvious aesthetic value, and preservation boards may not require their conservation.

But in any project, I see it as my responsibility to seek out what *is* inherently valuable in what exists and to use *that* to enhance an entire property. That is the key. We must find the elements that best capture the true character of the original and then let them lead the way. This allows us to preserve the often-intangible essence of the original even as we improve its more tangible aspects. The history and context of these homes thus become motivating forces and guiding principles but never straightjackets.

Channeling the intent of the architect who designed the house decades ago, I look to the best examples of other residences built in its particular period and style, and then design using the original vernacular, rather than creating a new language. At the same time, I seek not to exactly imitate what once was but to conceive what might have been.

Previously undervalued and neglected, the redone homes in this chapter convey a profound sense of nostalgia — something my own Wellesley property's former owner immediately recognized at that tag sale. But they also radiate a readiness to help their current residents create new memories. And that is what makes these buildings truly timeless. Although altered, the houses here remain true to the spirit of their pasts. They emerge from renovation better able to contribute to the greater good of their neighborhoods and the happiness of their owners.

ABOVE: Whether required by landmark regulations or not, I work to salvage and enhance the most architecturally significant elements of a house. The new wings of this Edgartown home, for example, honor the classic gambrel-roofed charm of the 1920s original.

OPPOSITE: Following its renovation, this 1930s English-country-manor-style property in Wellesley features a variety of new spaces for alfresco living and entertaining, as well as restored stonework on its front façade (BOTTOM LEFT).

57

ABOVE: Using the existing footprint, I re-imagined this 1973 cottage in Chatham on Cape Cod to appear as if it was once a collection of structures that were connected over time. Architectural elements such as the French doors and intricate pergola elevate the rear façade while providing ample opportunity for outdoor living.

RIGHT: In the Martha's Vineyard village of Vineyard Haven, a warren-like 1873 captain's home became an open, airy harbor-side retreat.

OPPOSITE: Staircases in historic homes can become finely detailed architectural elements to savor, rather than hide away.

A COTTAGE WITH ROOM TO GROW

Wellesley Farms, Massachusetts

MY WIFE AND I first fell in love with our Wellesley Farms house because of its decidedly non-suburban look and feel. From the 1920s through the '40s, Boston-based architect Royal Barry Wills designed some of the most romantic residences in New England, bringing traditional old-world design idioms — like our stonewalled English cottage — to the region. I'd long admired his houses' ability to transport you to another place and time. Not everyone appreciated their quirks, however, or their seeming resistance to adapt to contemporary life.

RIGHT: When expanding and renovating my 1936 English-countryside-inspired home in Wellesley Farms, just outside of Boston, I worked with the themes, materials, and scale of the existing building. My goal was to channel its original designer, New England architect Royal Barry Wills.

OPPOSITE: The rustic stone fireplace, wood floors, and mahogany countertops of the home's new combined kitchen and family room conjure Wills's sense of nostalgia.

ABOVE, LEFT: The home evokes the timelessness of pastoral pleasures, right down to its ivy-covered façade — and my 1960 Corvette in the driveway.

ABOVE, RIGHT: Using an antique Irish butcher block as a kitchen island provides the space with extra warmth.

When we bought the cottage, weeds had grown up around it, and the previous owners had replaced the original wood-shake roof with asphalt shingles. Its three bedrooms and two bathrooms, small by any standard, felt especially tiny given that our family then numbered six (and would soon grow to seven). But I saw something in the house — and its hilltop setting dotted with old-growth trees — that others failed to appreciate. Wills had a feeling for scale, materiality, and nostalgia that I share. I knew I could channel and elevate that, while enlarging and renovating the structure to accommodate us all.

After we bought it, I found the original plans for the building — titled "House for Mr. and Mrs. Myles Standish and Maid" — in the attic, and I immersed myself in the world of Wills and his work. Then I asked myself, "If it were 1936 and he'd had a larger program for this house, what would Royal Barry Wills have done?"

The answer, I decided, was to make the home look as if it had grown slowly, just as a real English cottage would have. I expanded the building from two thousand to four thousand square feet — adding wings to either side, extending the entrance, pushing the back out in three places — and created a carriage house from the base of the original one-story garage. But you'd never know it. Each relatively small addition steps back from the main house; the materials we used and fixtures we re-created seamlessly continue the story Wills started to tell; and our flower-planted window boxes and twinkling Christmas lights recall Currier & Ives. Thanks to our work's sensitivity to appropriate proportions, authentic craftsmanship, and romantic nostalgia — all inspired by Wills himself — the enriched home looks as natural in its setting as ever.

RIGHT: I reimagined a walnut-paneled 1960s addition at the rear of the house as a library, adding wood beams, French doors, and a limestone fireplace that would have made Wills proud.

ABOVE AND OPPOSITE: The antique beams,
V-groove paneling, and fireplace surround —
whose stones match those on the home's exterior
— allow the new master bedroom to look like it
also dates to 1936.

ABOVE: In addition to expanding the property's main house and carriage house, I added a second carriage house and this Amish-style entertaining barn. Its stone base matches that of the Wills buildings, while the board-and-batten cladding gives it a classic feel.

OPPOSITE: The entertaining barn's upper level opens to a bluestone terrace, the better for hosting warm-weather indoor-outdoor events. The new carriage house can be seen behind, nestled at the edge of the property.

ROYAL BARRY WILLS RECONSIDERED

Wellesley Farms, Massachusetts

WHILE MY OWN HOME was in fairly rough shape when I bought it, another Wills house I was privileged to work on in Wellesley had undergone even greater indignities. The grand 1941 center-hall red brick Georgian Colonial had suffered through unsympathetic additions and renovations that largely stripped it of its charm: anachronistic bay windows from the 1960s replaced double-hung casement fenestration, and rooms lay bare, stripped of nearly all molding and trim.

RIGHT: This 1941 Georgian Colonial in Wellesley, and also designed by Wills, required the removal of several insensitive 1960s interventions. Besides restoring the brick portion to its former glory, we expanded the home with several white-clapboard wings.

RIGHT: To minimize the additions' impact on the home's classic character, we altered the topography of the property, setting the carriage house wing, for example, down into the landscape.

FOLLOWING PAGES: Though actually two stories tall, the carriage house looks like a single-level guest cottage when seen from the inner courtyard.

Our task was to bring the main house back in line with Wills's design, and then use it to inspire a significantly more suitable expansion. A previous owner helped us in this endeavor, sharing decades of photos that showed the residence at its best, before the first renovations. With the client's endorsement — she, too, appreciated the often-undervalued Wills — we used these images to get to work. We removed two wings from the 1950s, replacing them with gambrel-roofed, white clapboard and red brick additions that grew out of Wills's keen understanding of traditional vernacular architecture, and we celebrated the craftsmanship of the primary façade, restoring original windows and framing them with bluestone lintels and brick soldier courses. A pair of new chimneys and a white-painted portico further elevate the entry and honor the past.

Inside, Wills's signature knotty-pine paneling, now painted, extends beyond the den — which today serves as the dining room — into several other spaces, including the new mudroom and kitchen. Adorned with rebuilt balustrades that exactly replicate those from 1941, the original staircase, meanwhile, leads to a reconfigured second floor. There, a new four-foot-wide beamed corridor connects bedrooms and bathrooms that both preserve Wills's sense of proportion and accommodate the needs of twenty-first-century living — just like the rest of the house.

THE JEWEL IN THE CHATHAM CROWN

Chatham, Cape Cod, Massachusetts

SITTING MAJESTICALLY atop a knoll on Shore Road — easily the most beautiful street in Chatham, if not all Cape Cod — this expansive shingle-style house takes the New England saltbox vernacular to unexpected heights. It had been a fixture on the harbor since its construction, back in 1910, but by the time we got the commission to renovate it, the original structure was failing, and ill-conceived mid-century additions had obscured its beauty.

RIGHT: The design of this house recreates — and significantly expands and enhances — a 1910 shingle-style single-gable residence that once stood on its site. Preserving that building proved impossible, sadly, but we honored its history with a new home that imagined a double-gabled version of the original.

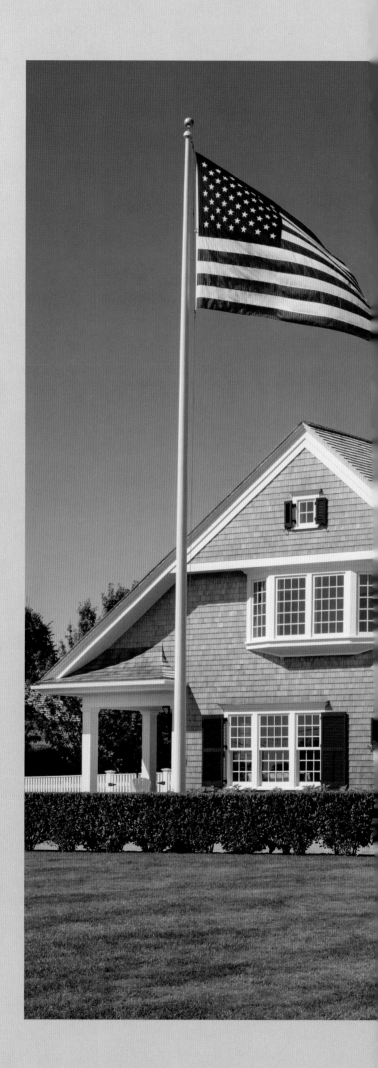

OPPOSITE: A mix of classically casual materials, such as antique brick floors and horizontal V-groove boards, with more formal elements, including heavy casing and molded paneling, clads the mudroom.

RIGHT: A framed artwork fills a niche above the mudroom's built-in chest of drawers, providing a dramatic focal point.

FOLLOWING PAGES: Once the living room, the large foyer functions as the heart of the home and provides views to the terrace, pool, and new cabana.

We planned to remove the addition and create an enlarged double-gabled house, connecting the historic building to a newly constructed mirror image of it. It soon became clear, however, that the century-old structure was too compromised to salvage. We had to tear it down.

At that point, we could have abandoned our plan — in fact, the clients considered doing so. But I felt a responsibility to the community to re-create this beloved historic house on its site. I explained this to the clients, convincing them of their home's public value and important role in Chatham. Recommitted to the greater good, they decided to continue on our intended path.

Using archival photos and the demolished remains as our guide, we lifted key details from the 1910 building: the layering of façade embellishments, the rhythm of fenestration, the foyer's fireplace and exposed joists. These helped capture the character of the original, whose spirit we then carried through the entire building, combining those elements with other materials and features characteristic of historic Chatham homes. Despite the unexpected demolition, this Cape Cod grand dame emerged enhanced and elevated, rooted in the past but reaching for the future.

ABOVE: A Dutch door in the beadboard-clad butler's pantry connects the kitchen to an outdoor dining terrace.

RIGHT: The simple clean lines of the kitchen, with its timeless wood floors and Carrera marble counters, take their inspiration from the service kitchens of older homes.

LEFT: Despite the grand scale of the master bathroom, V-groove paneling and multipaned windows maintain the cottage vernacular.

OPPOSITE: Taking aesthetic cues from the 1910 structure, one side of the property's new outbuilding serves as a pool cabana, the other as a carriage house.

FOLLOWING PAGES: The reimagined home captures the character of the original — borrowing key historic elements like the layering of façade embellishments and the rhythm of fenestration — while simultaneously celebrating its status as a contemporary summer home designed for indoor-outdoor living.

3

History Modernized

The modernists I studied in graduate school might disagree, but I'll say it anyway: in terms of aesthetics, there's nothing about classical architecture that's inherently at odds with contemporary living. In fact, I'd argue that traditional vernacular types — from Colonial to Victorian, Greek Revival to shingle style — are actually more appropriate to how people want to live today. Such buildings capture the romance and nostalgia of the idea of "hearth and home" better than any unornamented glass-and-steel box.

When it comes to their floor plans and interior spaces, however, historic houses often leave much to be desired. There are obvious issues, like small kitchens and even tinier bathrooms, and the absence of basements and closets. But subtle challenges exist as well: houses from the seventeenth through the early twentieth centuries often have warren-like configurations of rooms and clumsily mix private and public spaces. Both factors make for complicated, disjointed circulation and constrained spaces. Adding to the feeling of claustrophobia, these buildings tend to look inward rather than out: they rarely use large windows and glass doors to maximize views and natural light, and despite the prevalence of porches, they don't prioritize indoor-outdoor living.

The renovated historic homes in this chapter — and, indeed, those of nearly all the houses my firm works on — alleviate these problems. Containing the kind of interior spaces contemporary clients crave, they manifest an innovative, modern approach to space, one based on the design teachings of twentieth-century greats from the Bauhaus and beyond. Their open plans create flow and transparency, connect indoors with out, and can be adapted to accommodate fifty guests as comfortably as five.

All this is accomplished without sacrificing the fundamental antique character of a house. Instead, carefully considered period details and materials as well as authentically vintage finishes and fixtures, outfit the new, relatively contemporary interiors. That combination of old and new is the foundation of their timeless appeal.

To achieve open flow, I begin by designing interiors off a central spine. This axis connects the rooms of a house from front to back or side to side. More often than not, I create two perpendicular spines, with rooms opening onto one or both. Not to be confused with hallways, these spines are more like galleries, filled with light and art and meant to be lived in and enjoyed. They don't just connect rooms but serve as fully furnished gathering and entertaining areas themselves.

These spines pull you through a home, providing long views and enticing you to explore. Typically, each spine resolves itself in an alluring vista or other temptation: it may lead to a warmly lit kitchen or breakfast room, or a set of French doors offering glimpses of a lawn, pool, or beachfront that draws you outside. There, I build covered porches that act as alfresco rooms, with fireplaces and plush furnishings that enable the house to expand in warmer weather.

This expansion is vertical as well as horizontal. Dormered attics become commodious master suites or clerestories in double-height great rooms. Thanks to careful landscaping, semi-subterranean stories serve not as basements but as light-filled garden levels, with recreational space and guest quarters that give onto courtyards and patios. None of these transformations requires the building to balloon externally — it stays perfectly in scale with its vintage surroundings.

Modernist theory and thinking guide all our interiors, but we design them to be of a piece with a home's historic or historically motivated exterior and the context of its centuries-old neighbors. As a result, each timeless residence remains true to its original era, without requiring its occupants to live a period lifestyle.

In this home in West Chop, on Martha's Vineyard, the double-height great room (LEFT) links the first story to the second, where a repurposed stair landing (OPPOSITE) becomes usable living space.

REVIVING A GREEK REVIVAL

Edgartown Village Historic District,
Martha's Vineyard, Massachusetts

LIKE SO MANY OF MY CLIENTS, the family
that owns the Captain Consider Fisher House
in Edgartown, on Martha's Vineyard, wanted
a summer vacation home that would feel both
intimate and ready to entertain large groups.
To accommodate their extensive program and
still be sensitive to the building's past and its
vintage surroundings, we had to expand the
house greatly, while at the same time keeping
it in scale with its neighborhood. This posed a
substantial challenge, but we found a solution
in a scheme that nearly doubled the size of
the original early-nineteenth-century Greek
Revival cottage by adding a second historically
appropriate gabled structure connected to the
first by a breezeway.

RIGHT: Updating Edgartown's early-1800s
Captain Consider Fisher House for the twenty-
first century meant adding a matching, smaller-
scale Greek Revival gabled wing to the right of
the original. I connected them with a breezeway
and developed an interior scheme that erased
any distinction between old and new.

ABOVE: In centuries past, relatively expensive painted clapboard was used only on front façades, a precedent I followed here. I clad the back elevation — including the new service porch and mudroom entry on the left — in shingles.

OPPOSITE: For the original wing, I designed a historically accurate transom to replace an anachronistic barrel-vaulted portico over the front door.

The breezeway sits at the center of a new spine that runs from left to right on both the first and second stories, reorganizing circulation and opening up the formerly closed floor plan. On the main level, it serves as a large dining room, something the clients required. Because this is also a circulation space in the middle of the home, it avoids the stuffiness of a more formal, traditional dining room. It gets significant use, as residents and guests move from the entry halls and living room in the nineteenth-century building to the open kitchen and family room in the new one. People can't resist its six sets of French doors, which open front and back to covered porches. On the upper floor, the breezeway connects the master suite under the new gable with three additional bedrooms beneath the original roof. Again, this area is much more than a hallway, transforming instead into a bookshelf-lined library and gallery. Outfitted with two overstuffed sofas, this space is illuminated by dormers and by French doors that give onto a pair of decks.

Filled with light and life, the newly expanded and revived home maintains the spirit and charm of the original cottage, emulating its aesthetic in coffered ceilings, wide-plank wood floors, beadboard, and wainscoted walls used throughout. At the same time, it is unequivocally ready for modern living and entertaining.

LEFT: The front door opens to an entry hall, which features the stairs' original newel post, followed by an entry gallery.

OPPOSITE: In the butler's pantry, nickel hardware, antique hardwood flooring, and tall glass cabinets give the patina of age.

FOLLOWING PAGES: The homeowners had grown accustomed to twelve-foot ceilings in their primary residence, so I incorporated a ten-foot ceiling height while maintaining a historically accurate scale from the streetscape. In the kitchen, the height allows for additional cupboard space.

LEFT: Finished with six sets of French doors and a beamed ceiling, the breezeway serves as both a dining room and circulation space, connecting the entry and living room in the old wing to the new kitchen and family room.

FOLLOWING PAGES: The renovated house today blends indoors and out — on the first and second floors, nearly every room opens onto a large covered porch, deck, or balcony.

PATRICK AHEARN

A COTTAGE
BY THE SEA

Edgartown Village Historic District,
Martha's Vineyard, Massachusetts

THIS WHITE-CLAPBOARD Martha's Vineyard
cottage, commonly referred to as the Nunnepog
House, has a curious history. Originally built
three lots north of its current location, in the
1840s, it housed a series of prominent islanders
— among them a retired sea captain and, later, a
renowned shopkeeper — before being moved in
1950 to where it now sits. When we received the
commission to work on it, in 2013, the owners
were in a quandary: they loved the history of
their 2,250-square-foot home, but it failed
to take full advantage of its sea views, and it
struggled to accommodate their children and
guests in summer.

RIGHT: This 1840s Edgartown Greek Revival
features a stepped-back, smaller-scale addition
to the left of the original cottage, as well as a new
garden level. The remastered interior, meanwhile,
makes modern living and entertaining easy.

OPPOSITE: A new carriage house, located just beyond the addition, echoes the Greek Revival details of the original façade.

RIGHT: The spar-varnished beadboard ceiling of the covered porch hints at the formality of the interiors.

Our proposal was to significantly but subtly expand the building, adding a lower garden level and a ground-floor wing, as well as opportunities for indoor-outdoor living. To preserve the historic scale and integrity of the house, we designed the new lower portion to be invisible from the street, and we set the new wing back considerably.

This attention to scale and history continues within, although the redone interiors provide a modern sense of space and improved views. The garden level houses guest rooms and a multipurpose game room whose heavily cased fireplace and beadboard ceiling add a sense of atmosphere that is anything but basement-like. Four pairs of French doors and a trio of additional windows open to a bluestone patio and harbor vistas. Above, in the new wing, we added a master suite with a private courtyard. Even more innovatively, we removed the first-floor ceiling in much of the original house to create a double-height space, one that didn't require changing the building's outward appearance. This large yet intimate great room — finished with such classic details as a mahogany-stained beadboard ceiling — opens to a kitchen and a dining room. We styled the latter, which is surrounded on three sides by windows, to look like a former open-air porch that was eventually enclosed with glass — an architectural narrative typical of the Vineyard.

The house remains intimate in scale and timeless in appeal as it honors its harbor-side location and how its owners live.

OPPOSITE: To create a grand, double-height great room without affecting the modest exterior appearance of the home, we removed the second-story floor plate. We finished the ceiling with mahogany-stained beadboard to reinforce the sense of height.

RIGHT: A custom-designed, traditionally detailed mantle adds to the classic sensibility of the great room.

FOLLOWING PAGES: Open to the kitchen and dining room, with sweeping water views, the great room can easily accommodate large gatherings. A sense of intimacy still defines it, however, preventing a feeling of emptiness when only the homeowners are in residence.

LEFT: I designed the kitchen with the homeowners' passion for cooking and hosting in mind. Optimized for entertaining, it reflects the formal tone of the great room.

PATRICK AHEARN

OPPOSITE: I designed the dining room to look like a former open-air porch that was subsequently enclosed. Mahogany trim and beadboard ceilings visually connect the great room to the various spaces off it, even as their lower heights reinforce the sense that they are distinct areas.

OPPOSITE AND ABOVE: Occupying the first floor of the new wing, the master suite enjoys coveted marsh and harbor views from the large windows in both its elegantly detailed bathroom and grandly gabled bedroom. In the latter, a Palladian window creates a particularly romantic effect.

The renovated house and re-landscaped property (ABOVE, TOP) provides abundant opportunities for alfresco fun: from the secret garden outside the master suite (ABOVE, BOTTOM), to a guest suite's private patio (RIGHT), to the pool and fireplace porch off the great room (FOLLOWING PAGES).

FROM DARKNESS TO LIGHT

Osterville, Cape Cod, Massachusetts

As a beach house, this grand gambrel-roofed, shingle-style house in Cape Cod's Osterville seemed like a missed opportunity. Although built on Nantucket Sound, it didn't make the most of its waterfront location. A jumble of dark, Gothic-feeling interiors provided only glimpses of the sea, and it offered meager access to the multi-acre yard and sand and surf beyond.

RIGHT: Once a warren of dark, inward-facing rooms — not to mention half its current size — this Cape Cod house now lives up to the promise of its waterfront location. The reimagined home boasts long views, abundant natural light, and plentiful indoor-outdoor living areas.

RIGHT: I seamlessly added new wings on either side of the original house, maintaining the shingle-style building's timeless and quintessential Cape character.

The clients also required additional space from the nineteenth-century structure: several more children's bedrooms, a master suite, a home office, and a four-car carriage house, to name only part of the program. We increased the square footage by adding a new wing to mirror the original house. This came close to doubling the building's size and simultaneously created implied symmetry that maintained the exterior's historic nature, a theme carried through inside.

We simplified circulation within the floor plan, while letting in more light and providing generous outdoor access. The original house featured a double-height great room whose expanses of dark wood felt poorly suited to the beach. We kept the space but minimized its heavy woodwork and lightened the color of the remaining trim. This created a bright, airy ambiance that didn't sacrifice character. The room now feels like a more appropriate and functional heart of the home: on the ground level, a central spine runs through the space, connecting the lively kitchen and its adjacent pantry, breakfast room, and morning room with the more formal and private den, office, and master suite. Upstairs, a U-shaped open gallery surrounds the great room, connecting six bedrooms and a second den.

While paying careful attention to the home's past, we reversed its focus, enabling it to look outside instead of in. Now, sun flows through large windows and French doors, and rooms have direct access to new porches, terraces, and decks. This eases the transition from indoors to out, inviting residents and guests to enjoy the pool, yard, and waterfront. This grand seaside residence stands as a perfectly timeless beach house made for contemporary summer living.

ABOVE: A small formal garden provides a quiet, intimate spot for reading or reflection.

RIGHT: The smaller of the two new stepped-back wings, this one on the building's west side, hosts a secondary entrance below a deck finished with a classic Chippendale railing.

PATRICK AHEARN

OPPOSITE: Once rather Gothic and inward facing, the double-height great room now features preserved, albeit lightened, woodwork, plus an interior window that lets in sun from an upstairs bedroom and French doors that connect the space to the outdoors.

ABOVE: Accessible from either the screened porch or the den, the study provides a warm retreat from family activities.

BELOW: Stainless-steel appliances give the kitchen a timeless look, while mahogany-stained cabinets make the island feel like a piece of freestanding furniture.

OPPOSITE: Details consistent with the spirit of the original home — including open shelving, a skirted sink, and classic bin pulls — elevate the butler's pantry.

OPPOSITE: Period wall sconces, honed Carrera marble countertops, and a petite dressing table convey a sense of Cape Cod history in the master suite's dressing area.

ABOVE: Traditional materials prevent the master bathroom from seeming overtly modern, though its large size and dual vanities meet contemporary needs.

PATRICK AHEARN

ABOVE: Easing the transition from indoors to out, the great room opens to a brick-floored, shingle-clad screened porch through a set of three French doors.

OPPOSITE: A new beach folly — located halfway between the house and the sand, and designed in the same vernacular as the main structure — serves as a playful changing room.

FOLLOWING PAGES: The design elements of the restored, expanded, and reorganized home draw you through its interiors, and finally, outside. The screened porch's antique brick flooring, for example, continues onto the back terrace, connecting the two spaces and leading to the lawn beyond.

4

History Imagined

Whenever I want to introduce my work to prospective
clients, I take them on a tour of my family's property on
Martha's Vineyard. Guiding them through the three New
England vernacular buildings set on a tight parcel of land
in Edgartown's historic district, I tell them the story
of our home.

The two-and-a-half-floor main house dates to the 1790s, when a midshipman built the center-hall Federal Colonial. In the early 1800s, he attached a barn to the back, with horse stalls on one side. When the family outgrew the original residence, at the end of the nineteenth century, the barn was transformed into living space, and the stalls were repurposed for food storage and preparation. Shortly afterward, livery stables were added at the property's rear.

Today, the ground level of the 1790 structure contains the most formal spaces — a living room and a dining room — with bedrooms on the second floor and in the dormered former attic. The wood-beamed barn behind became our double-height family room, flanked by a modern kitchen where the stalls once were and a covered porch. As for the livery stables, they now serve as a three-car carriage house that provides space for large parties, its upper level holding a guest suite. In between the buildings, an area previously used for livestock and laundry hosts a pool and landscaped courtyard.

These tours typically end in that courtyard, with clients remarking on the historic details of the architecture and the backstory. They all have the same question: "How did you manage such a massive restoration?"

And then I have to come clean: "It's not a renovation," I confess. "I built the house from scratch in 2003. I invented that entire story to help me create a design that would be believable."

After that, I usually get hired.

When creating classically inspired new-build houses, I consider myself a storyteller as much as an architect. For every project, I write a detailed script that explains a home's origins, how it grew through the years, and why it was built in a certain style. This imagined narrative — grounded in real research and deep knowledge — allows me to combine my respect for architectural history and context with the requirements of twenty-first-century living. The result is a design whose timelessness pleases the house's occupants, preserves the character of the neighborhood, and contributes to the greater good of the community.

If my work has a signature, it is not an overarching aesthetic quality but rather the way my concern for historically appropriate scale and authentic style manifests itself in every house I design.

Centuries-old properties, especially those in New England, often consisted of several relatively compact structures built through the years. My narratives talk about the addition over time of different architectural elements. This lets me split the large, complicated programs of contemporary clients into several pieces, across a handful of interrelated smaller buildings. These individual components remain in context with their historic surroundings better than a single massive monolithic mansion could. Just as important, the ensembles make the most of indoor and outdoor spaces and provide a variety of discrete environments in which to congregate and celebrate, relax and recharge.

Developing a script based on local history helps me select a style for a property that is appropriate to its sense of place, ensuring that a home's look and feel are true to nearby precedents. I use the narrative to peg the imagined past of a house to its particular place and then to a particular period — and sometimes even to a particular person, like my invented midshipman. I then develop the aesthetic from these specifics, choosing materials, finishes, and fixtures to make the story convincing. The details are key.

The narratives also allow me to present schemes to clients in a captivating and relatable way. Doing so humanizes both the process and the final product, which helps makes these buildings successful and appealing. Rooted in their sites and in sync with their surroundings, the appropriately scaled and authentically styled new homes in this chapter feel as if they'd stood where they are for centuries. But even as their imagined histories link them to the past, they engage fully with the present and encourage their occupants to look to the future.

To make a newly built house feel authentic, I develop a script that explains the design in historically accurate terms — a vintage livery stable turned residence (ABOVE AND RIGHT), for example, or an old farmhouse and barn added onto over time (OPPOSITE).

INVENTING CHARACTER ON MARTHA'S VINEYARD

Edgartown Village Historic District,
Martha's Vineyard, Massachusetts

IN THE CASE OF my family's Edgartown home, the idea of a late-eighteenth-century midshipman — representing a group who resided on the island at the time and built houses like ours — drove the narrative and led me to many of the design's most salient details. Lacking the financial means of captains, who constructed painted-clapboard harbor-front dwellings, this sailor would have used inexpensive shingles for the exterior, adding twelve-over-twelve small-paned windows like the ones we put in, as well as our broad front door with English bubble glass and granite-slab steps.

RIGHT: For my Edgartown home, I imagined that a midshipman built the Federal Colonial in the 1790s then renovated over the years, eventually turning an attached barn into living space and adding a livery stable behind.

RIGHT: Thinking the midshipman had a penchant for Greek Revival, I added large columns and an entablature to the living room, which I thought of as the "former" parlor.

The midshipman's home would have had the wide-plank pine floors with cut-faced nails that ours has. In addition, seeking to make some extra money, he might have opened a tavern on his ground floor, which is why our dining room sports wood-paneling, rough-hewn beams, and a Rumford fireplace to greet you as you enter through the foyer.

Within the home, the program was driven not by fiction but by the real-life requirements of our contemporary existence, over which I layered the midshipman story and the style and scale it suggested. Neither the formal areas nor the five bedrooms needed to be big, so I nestled them within the smaller proportions of the 1790 building. We wanted an expansive, open family room and kitchen, however, so they went in the barn and adjacent horse stalls. Our desire for a guest suite and large carriage house guided me to the livery stable. I put this at the rear of our long, thin plot of land, both because it was historically correct for it to sit on the commercial thoroughfare the property backs onto and because it saved us from driving down or parking on our quiet, narrow street.

Using this livery stable to bookend the site gave us the privacy we craved for our alfresco space. With the livery stable's pergola at one end and the main house's covered porch at the other, the back lawn became a courtyard — the perfect indoor-outdoor room for a new-old house designed for summertime family fun.

ABOVE: I styled the dining room as a walnut-paneled, timber-beamed tavern, a venue the midshipman might have opened to make extra money.

OPPOSITE: In my script, our family room is in the old barn — complete with trussed ceiling and beadboard walls — which became part of the main house in the early 1800s.

ABOVE AND OPPOSITE: The kitchen, which
opens from the family room, fills a space I
conceived as the barn's horse stalls. Its vintage
beams echo the trusses of the family room,
and the wide-plank antique floorboards extend
throughout the house.

ABOVE: In the breakfast nook off the family room, a barn-appropriate Dutch door leads to the courtyard's swimming pool and carriage house.

OPPOSITE: The twelve-over-twelve window in the second-floor writing nook overlooks the charming lane on which the house sits.

The authentically styled master suite — in the "original" 1790s building — features post-and-beam details in the bedroom (ABOVE), beadboard paneling in the bathroom (RIGHT), and French doors leading to a private deck with views of the pool courtyard (OPPOSITE).

ABOVE AND OPPOSITE: The carriage house allowed the backyard to become a courtyard. Its first floor proves perfect for entertaining, as the swinging arched doors open onto a pergola-covered brick terrace with views to the pool. The second level, meanwhile, holds a guest suite.

A GREEK REVIVAL RETREAT FOR A BLENDED FAMILY

Edgartown Village Historic District,
Martha's Vineyard, Massachusetts

THIS EDGARTOWN HOUSE had to accommodate a low-key Ohio-based creative couple and their newly blended Brady Bunch–style set of six kids, most of whom lived on their own but would be assembling from time to time on the Vineyard. The clients wanted something modest that would feel intimate with just a few people in residence but not overcrowded when full. This meant having spaces large and open enough to fit the whole family, plus others petite and enclosed enough to provide privacy. A tall order, any way you sliced it.

RIGHT: For homeowners that required plenty of space but also wanted a house that felt humble and intimate, I designed an ensemble of several historically appropriate structures — including this street-front carriage house — that I imaged had been built and added onto over the years.

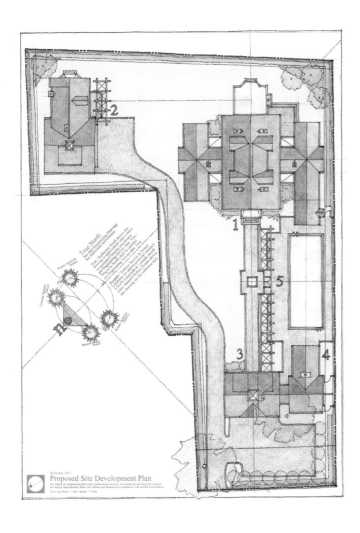

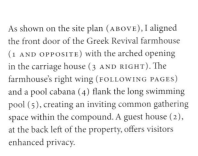

As shown on the site plan (ABOVE), I aligned the front door of the Greek Revival farmhouse (1 AND OPPOSITE) with the arched opening in the carriage house (3 AND RIGHT). The farmhouse's right wing (FOLLOWING PAGES) and a pool cabana (4) flank the long swimming pool (5), creating an inviting common gathering space within the compound. A guest house (2), at the back left of the property, offers visitors enhanced privacy.

In the end, slicing up their program and allocating different parts of it among several buildings proved the perfect solution. I developed a script based on the actual past of the large, early-eighteenth-century Greek Revival farmhouse across the street from my clients' L-shaped plot. Like that historic home, this new-build, I imagined, had been constructed in the 1830s on extensive acreage and added onto over time. The other elements, several of them closer to the road, had been built later: the carriage house that conceals the main structure from the street in the late 1800s; the adjacent pool cabana in the 1930s, when alfresco parties were the rage; and the guest house and its attendant garage at the back left in the 1910s, when cars came to the island.

This timeline led me to the styles I included — Greek Revival for the "original" portion, shingle for what came "later." It also kept the structures in scale with the smaller houses in the neighborhood, even as it helped me accommodate all the required spaces. The main house has an expansive family room, plus seven bedrooms. Two are in a stepped-back one-story wing designed to look like an addition, a mirror image of which on the other side holds a kitchen and dining room. The garage contains two additional bedrooms plus more living space, and the carriage house and cabana offer more sleep and play areas.

The campus-like configuration creates a variety of private and public alfresco rooms — around the pool and cabana, between the main house and garage, guest house, on porches, under pergolas — that further expand the house and encourage the easy living and entertaining this very contemporary family desired.

OPPOSITE: Mirroring the farmhouse's right wing, the pool cabana features a gabled porch and an outdoor fireplace, adding warmth to outdoor entertaining.

ABOVE: Detailed, full-height paneling and beach pine floors lend an air of authenticity to the foyer, drawing guests into the home and, just as important, into the world of the building's imagined history.

LEFT: I designed the dining area to appear as if it was once a porch that was later enclosed with windows.

OPPOSITE: Adjacent to the breakfast room, the vaulted, beamed ceiling lends a fitting farmhouse air to the kitchen.

ABOVE: A set of French doors connects the casual breakfast room, with its comfortable banquette seating, to a covered porch and the pool.

PATRICK AHEARN

RIGHT: The weathered-shingle wings on either side of the "original" white-clapboard farmhouse, as well as the one-story dining room in the "former" porch, serve to break down the size of the structure, making the large home appear smaller, and as a result, significantly more timeless.

FOLLOWING PAGES: Dividing the homeowner's extensive program across several buildings provided the space they needed, plus the flexibility and privacy they craved. It also kept the various pieces of the house in scale with the historic neighborhood.

PATRICK AHEARN

WEATHERING
THE STORM

Herring Creek Farm,
Martha's Vineyard, Massachusetts

ALTHOUGH THIS VINEYARD property is a
single building rather than a compound, I still
designed it by creating a historic narrative. This
script gave rise to a shingle-style vernacular
that could meet the demands of the clients'
modern program. Comprising 210 acres of
farm- and grassland within the waterfront
Katama plains region, Herring Creek Farm
was redeveloped as a private residential
enclave with just a handful of homes, each
a maximum of seventy-five hundred square
feet, no basements or outbuildings permitted.
This particular plot of seventeen acres was a
significant investment for my clients — a rather
formal couple with three school-age children
— and they wanted a home commensurate with
the commitment it represented.

RIGHT: My script for this H-shaped gambrel-
roofed waterfront home, in Edgartown's
pastoral Katama plains, took inspiration from
the stories behind the Gilded Age mansions
that sprang up along the Northeast's Atlantic
Coast in the late 1800s.

I reflected on the site and its constraints, together with the clients' program and personality, and wove a tale of a country house built in 1895, during the height of the Gilded Age. Back then, grand H-shaped, gambrel-roofed cottages were in vogue on large ocean plots from the Hamptons to Newport to Maine. In my telling, this one hosted decades of posh parties until the hurricane of 1938, one of the island's worst, rendered it uninhabitable. I imagined the house sat as a boarded-up shell until my clients bought it and hired me to give it a renewed lease on life.

Our fictional restoration made a new house within the old, turning the servants' wing into a three-car carriage house wing with an open kitchen and a family room facing the water behind. Arrayed across the middle of the H — which contains the formal living and dining rooms and a grand double-height staircase — are a study, a garden room, and an in-law apartment. On the dormered second floor are five bedrooms, including a commodious master suite with its own deck. Each room feels different, though related, which lends the home a sense of age, as if it had developed over the course of a century.

The house's intimacy, warmth, and romance come from its classical detailing and shape, which make it appear smaller than it is. This historic character conveys a sense of hearth and home, from the second-floor flowerboxes and seven fireplaces to the wainscoted walls and twinned rear porches that look out onto grass-covered farmland and crashing ocean waves.

BELOW AND RIGHT: The paneling, moldings, and custom mantel of the living room exude a sense of richness and sophistication equal to that of the façade's columned, balconied portico.

PATRICK AHEARN

BELOW: Beadboard paneling and Delft tiles extend into the breakfast area, where they add character and romance to a period-perfect Rumford fireplace.

OPPOSITE: The overmantel, wainscoting, and entablature in the dining room continue both the column motif and the use of highly detailed millwork.

ABOVE AND OPPOSITE: I designed the summer living room — with its arched limestone mantel, marble floors, and lattice-covered walls and ceiling — as an ode to Palm Beach, where the homeowners spend much of their time.

ABOVE: The elegant master bedroom, finished with three-quarter-height wainscoting and hardwood floors, overlooks Herring Creek Farm and the Atlantic Ocean in the distance.

OPPOSITE: The master suite's carefully rendered decorative elements extend to the bathroom, whose soaking tub takes advantage of natural light.

RIGHT: I positioned the pool to the southwest side of the house, preserving the water views from the rear of the home and keeping the back lawn open for entertaining.

FOLLOWING PAGES: The value of an H-shaped house goes deeper than its aesthetic. Because its various wings conceal one another, the form allows a relatively large home to appear smaller than it is. The wings can also be used to create various indoor-outdoor spaces.

5

History Reinterpreted

Although the vast majority of my clients come to me
because they want to create a house that looks and
feels as if it had stood on its site for centuries, now and
again homeowners request that we create something
that is connected less to the past and more to their own
particular aesthetic and contemporary way of living.
With these properties, the balance I always seek between
preservation and innovation is weighted more toward
the latter, but a sensitivity toward history still plays a
significant role.

ABOVE: Certain homes require more, rather than less, deviation from history to meet the aesthetic and programmatic needs of their owners — a porte-cochère cut through the middle of a gambrel (TOP), for example, or a series of small, densely positioned gables across a roofline (BOTTOM). But even in these cases, I strive to remain as sensitive to the past as possible.

OPPOSITE, TOP: Thanks to its oversailing eaves, intricate lattice work, and arched carriage doors, this companion building to a home in Edgartown combines the concept of a gatehouse, as the first introduction to the property, with that of a carriage house.

OPPOSITE, BOTTOM: This Wellesley home extrapolates the vernacular of a classically modest and petite Cape Cod into a 6,500-square-foot house with an extensive program. Designing the building to be low to the ground and deploying a U-shaped floor plan keep the scale seeming true to historic precedents.

Such projects usually require greater reinterpretation of local precedents and historic antecedents than others. Their designs, however, still stem from my deep respect for and knowledge of New England's classical vernacular architecture. What I've learned from these houses is that you can get very playful with the past, as long as you take it seriously. In other words, you've got to know the rules to break the rules — or at least bend some of them.

The design of the homes gathered in this chapter definitely asked me to play with precedent and bend a few rules. More often than not, this was because the magnitude of the clients' program couldn't be contained by the most traditional models. Other times, those traditional styles didn't appeal to the clients' aesthetic or jibe with their lifestyle. These clients still sought a certain timelessness but conveyed in a different, and often more modern, way. They commissioned my firm because they appreciated how we think about scale and context, about the space between buildings, and about the greater good of the communities in which we work.

Perhaps unsurprisingly, the design of these homes is not without challenges. Making this sort of architecture — structures that push the envelope of historic authenticity but still feel appropriate and of a piece with their surroundings — requires as much if not more careful consideration and sleight of hand than I usually deploy.

Here as in my other projects, I find that scripting helps tremendously. Based on the program or the clients' aesthetic — and often both — I seek out a particularly appropriate period from the history of a place and then spin a story based on that reality. This narrative-driven process lets me reconcile past and present.

A heightened sensitivity to scale also informs these projects, especially when they grow very large. Breaking an expansive façade into several pieces helps make an elevation appear more approachable and welcoming. Using grander trim, moldings, and other details that are in proportion with the overall size of the building helps too. Thoughtful detailing goes a long way toward masking innovation and reinterpretation that might otherwise appear ahistorical.

Because the interiors I design tend to be born out of modernist thinking regarding flow, openness, light, and a sense of expansiveness, the floor plans of the houses in this chapter share themes with those chronicled elsewhere in the book. Most notable are their use of central spines to connect rooms, and the ways in which alfresco living is facilitated through the connection of indoor with outdoor areas. Although their finishes may make them appear older, the homes' interiors feel entirely contemporary, accommodating the sorts of living spaces people want today.

The following pages highlight just how flexible vernacular architecture can be, proving that a newly built house can look historic but live modern. These homes demonstrate that although strict traditionalism is often called for, it is hardly the only way to design. Innovation adds value when architects work in historic styles, as long as they don't disrespect what came before.

ABOVE: Though neither treatment is strictly typical of historic homes, I often use significant archways to mark the transitions between reception halls that open directly into living spaces (LEFT), and I will juxtapose casual beadboard paneling with more formal moldings and trim (RIGHT). These elements help create an atmosphere that feels both free-flowing and ordered, rustic and refined — and therefore, much more in keeping with how people want to live right now.

OPPOSITE: Twenty-first-century pool cabanas — with fireplaces, kitchenettes, and walls of folding glass doors — can seem like they have nothing to do with the past, but careful attention to details ensures that they remain connected to their historic context.

AN OPULENT TAKE ON TURN-OF-THE-CENTURY STYLE

Wellesley Hills, Massachusetts

EVERYTHING ABOUT THIS family home in the historic Boston suburb of Wellesley had to bespeak grandeur. The scope of the program was large: the owners wanted the house to include the amenities of a modern resort, allowing their extended family to visit for long periods without having to leave the property. The clients also desired a residence with a majestic appearance that would convey a sense of importance. Creating a home that felt like a luxurious country inn, even as it remained intimate and in scale with its suburban surroundings, was no small feat.

RIGHT: This large and luxe Wellesley home departs from the more intimate scale of much historic architecture. It recalls the grand Cliff Walk estates of Newport, Rhode Island, however, and all its proportions remain internally consistent. This allows it to feel both appropriate and timeless.

ABOVE: I broke down the overall scale of the home in several ways: I clad the ground floor in New England fieldstone and the upper levels in splayed shingles, I modulated the depth of various elements of the façade, and I made the flanking wings only one-story tall.

OPPOSITE: The highly articulated details of all the monumental architectural elements — including the copper-roofed bay windows, the limestone-framed arched entry, the bracketed eaves, and the significant chimneys — further help to break down the scale of the house.

Added to the mix was the requirement that the design follow the principles of the traditional Hindu system of architecture Vastu Shastra. This meant working within certain strictures: the house needed to be set in the acreage's southwest quadrant. The formal entrance had to be the tallest one and located on the building's left side. Fire, water, and cooking elements all had to be oriented in certain directions.

To accommodate the clients' many needs, I chose as a historic precedent the turn-of-the-twentieth-century Cliff Walk estates of Newport, Rhode Island, whose expansiveness and splendor was in line with what the clients desired. From this, I developed a double-gabled scheme clad in stone and shingles, with stepped-back wings, all of which helped de-emphasize the home's heft. Keeping the building's proportions internally consistent, if not quite human scaled, I designed substantial exterior details, like fourteen-foot-tall columns, ten-foot-high doors, a monumental twelve-foot-high Romanesque archway at the entrance, and weighty trim and moldings.

Inside, ceilings are ten feet high, and one commodious space gives way to another along two central spines. The lower level holds a basketball court, arcade, and grown-up gathering spaces, while the top floor has a grandparents' suite. Throughout, detailing again makes the difference, adding a sense of intimacy that mitigates the size. This gave the clients what they wanted and still respected the neighborhood context.

ABOVE: The seven-and-a-half-foot-tall Richardson Romanesque entryway (TOP) establishes a theme of arches that continues into the entry gallery (BOTTOM) and extends throughout the circulation spaces of the entire residence.

RIGHT: The carefully crafted details in the great room include full-height paneling, floor-to-ceiling windows, French doors topped with glass transoms, and significant ceiling beams and moldings — all of which imbue this primary space with richness.

ABOVE: The sequential arches and pilasters
of the entry gallery, one of the home's most
significant architectural tours de force, resolve
themselves in a pair of glass-paned mahogany
doors that open to the library.

OPPOSITE: The full grandeur of the library only
reveals itself when the eye is drawn up from the
mahogany-paneled walls to the intricate details
of the vaulted ceiling.

RIGHT: The linear arrangement of the pergola, water feature, and multiple options for alfresco lounging and dining create an outdoor living room that reinforces the length and formality of the rectangular pool.

FOLLOWING PAGES: Conceived as something akin to a luxurious boutique resort — a place where the homeowners and members of their extended family could spend long stretches of time without ever having to leave — this private oasis provides extensive opportunities for rest and relaxation, gatherings of groups large and small, and hosting events both formal and informal, indoors and out.

A VINEYARD HOME PUTS ITS BEST FAÇADE FORWARD

Edgartown, Martha's Vineyard, Massachusetts

THIS FIVE-BEDROOM, year-round home on a meadowed hill in Edgartown, on Martha's Vineyard, at first looks like it adheres quite closely to classical vernacular. Its construction, however, departed from tradition in subtle but significant ways. This was due in large part to the specifics of the setting, overlooking Eel Pond and the ocean beyond. The sandy road the property sits on separates it from the pond and sea. Accordingly, the side of the building with the best water views had to be the elevation facing the street. It would be the most publicly visible to passersby, who would generally perceive it as the front of the house. The clients, however, saw this as the back of their home — and rightfully so — wanting it to have walls of windows and layers of porches and decks to take advantage of the views from the rooms they planned to use most.

RIGHT: The street-side façade of this Martha's Vineyard home looks toward the ocean. As a result, I broke with tradition to orient its front door to the back of the property. This kept the rear elevation free to celebrate the ocean views, which I took advantage of with walls of windows and glass doors, as well as porches and terraces.

ABOVE: Because the front of the home faces away from the street, the cobblestone-edged pea-stone driveway curves around the house from the road, culminating in a motor court at the formal entrance.

RIGHT: After walking on antique stone pavers casually set in the grass in an irregular pattern, one enters the home through a multilight front door. The interior finishes recall the grand shingle-style homes of the turn of the last century, but the open, free-flowing spaces encourage contemporary island living.

Our innovative solution centered on incorporating elements into this rear water-facing elevation that would allow it to read as a front façade, with all the symmetry and logic you'd expect from the street-facing side of a shingle-style manor from the late 1800s. What's behind these walls, however, is not an entry hall flanked by a formal dining room and parlor, but a great room that opens to a wood-paneled study and covered porch in one wing and an open kitchen and beadboard-walled family room in the other.

You'd never know that from the treatment of the exterior, however. We massaged the details and trim on the rear of the H-shaped gambrel-roofed building so that the French doors leading to the back porch look more like main entrance doors dividing a glass-enclosed foyer from the front stoop. Similarly, the water-facing living room takes on the appearance of a covered front porch. The white-balustrade-lined decks above — a vital but not truly traditional element — appear entirely in keeping with the scheme, marching across the entire elevation and lending it an authentic formality that makes the entire ensemble a convincing success.

PATRICK AHEARN

ABOVE: The entry foyer leads directly into the great room through the opening on the right, while also serving as the central hub in one of the home's two main spines.

RIGHT: Bookended by dueling brick-faced fireplaces (only one of which is seen here), the curving rear wall of the great room opens through a set of French doors onto a bluestone terrace and covered porch with its own fireplace.

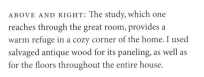
ABOVE AND RIGHT: The study, which one reaches through the great room, provides a warm refuge in a cozy corner of the home. I used salvaged antique wood for its paneling, as well as for the floors throughout the entire house.

OPPOSITE: Because the layout of the home's informal gathering spaces is largely open, I deployed deeply recessed entry portals — like this one between the great room and the kitchen — to reinforce the sense of transition as one moves through the house from one room to the next.

ABOVE: The large, entertaining-ready kitchen centers on a pair of islands — the one in the foreground is conceived for serving and hosting; the other is designed for prep work, washing dishes, and cooking.

OPPOSITE: The home's primary stairway sits in a hidden tower located off the entry gallery.

RIGHT, TOP AND BOTTOM: The master suite blends formal details with elements of seaside vernacular architecture, including a brick-faced fireplace, three-quarter-height wainscoting, beadboard cathedral ceilings, and elliptical clerestory windows.

FOLLOWING PAGES: Although this street-side elevation doesn't contain the home's primary entrance, the arrangement of its central terrace and French doors, as well as the symmetry of its gambrel wings, offer the suggestion of a front façade. This is the major innovation of the house's design.

RIGHT: The white-painted columns, wood-burning brick fireplace, and groupings of comfortable furniture reinforce the conception of this bluestone-floored covered porch as an extension of the home's interiors.

FOLLOWING PAGES: A view from the widow's walk reveals the various outdoor rooms activating the side of the campus-like property that doesn't face the water. These include the motor court, a secondary terrace off the carriage house, and a pool area with an adjacent cabana.

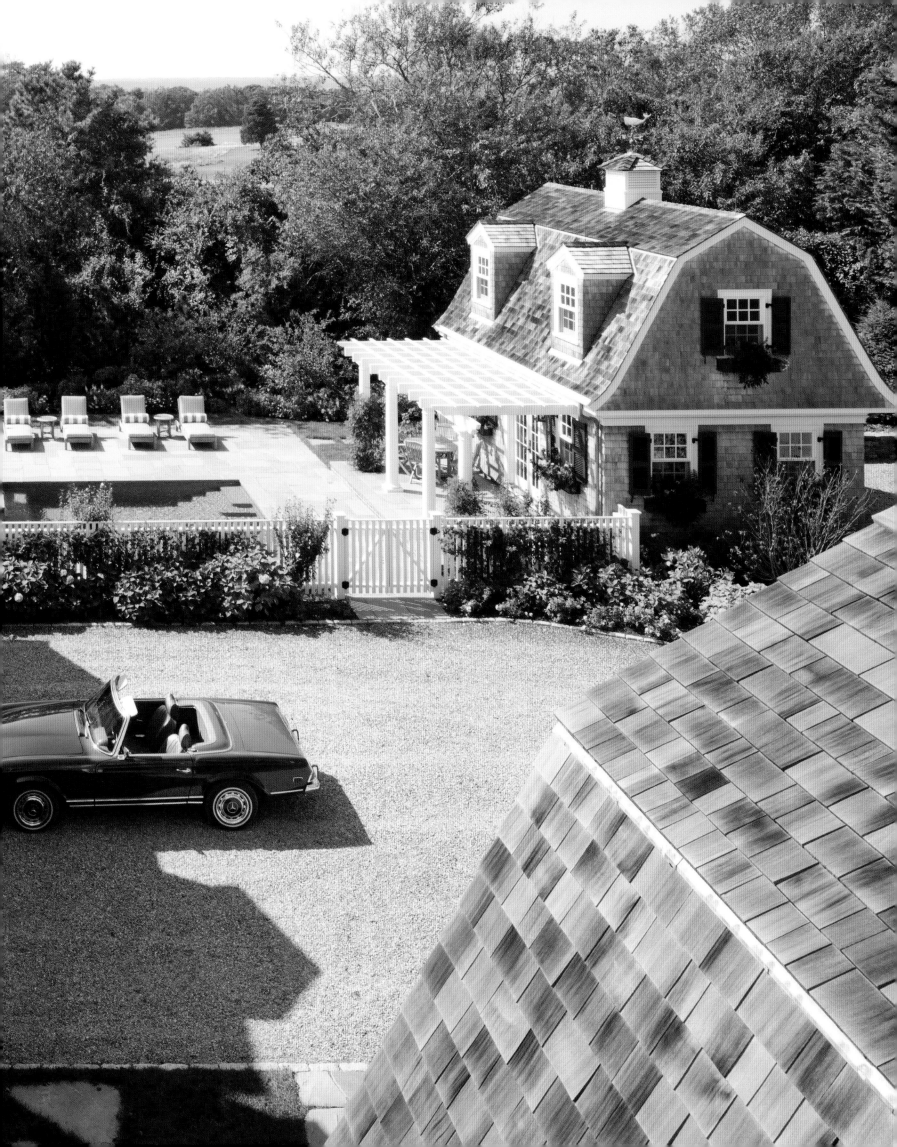

MADE FOR TV

Edgartown, Martha's Vineyard,
Massachussets

IF THIS HOUSE LOOKS FAMILIAR, that may be because you've seen it on television. I designed the HGTV Dream Home 2015 in Edgartown, on Martha's Vineyard, as a single-level house with three bedrooms all within an intimate 3,200 square feet. Its open plan, conducive to indoor-outdoor living, had to include a great room with chef's kitchen, a cozy master suite with a lavish bath, and a good-sized garage. The project had to be completed on a fast-track schedule and kept within a limited budget.

RIGHT: Based on the vernacular of the abandoned turn-of-the-century fishing-camp shacks found in the area, the traditional exterior of this home in Edgartown's Katama plains belies the open-plan, free-flowing spaces found within. The beauty of this relatively simple, timeless house is that it could just as easily be re-clad in any number of other architectural aesthetics.

RIGHT: I conceived the great room as the primary gathering space of the seasonal fisherman who once stayed here. To update and enhance it from this imagined humble beginning, I added beadboard paneling and clerestory dormers, creating a bright and airy retreat. The stone fireplace and antique-beamed ceiling, meanwhile, hint at the history of the home's fictional past.

Other than these programmatic and logistical demands, there were no other requirements, leaving me free to develop the aesthetic as I desired. In selecting an appropriate vernacular and reinterpreting it to meet the needs of contemporary living, I took inspiration from the property's location near South Beach and the former farms of the Katama plains. In the early 1900s, locals built one-room hunting and fishing shacks there. I imagined I'd come across a trio of these gable-roofed structures: a larger one in the middle, with a stone fireplace, and two smaller ones on either side, for storing gear and curing meat. In my concept, I used breezeways and porches to connect these three "found" buildings into one new structure designed for twenty-first-century residents.

A dormered double-height great room and kitchen sit in the central white-clapboard section, with the wood-beamed master suite in the shingled wing on the right and two smaller beadboard-ceilinged bedrooms and a garage on the left. Four terraces surround it, with a pair of chimneys and a small cupola on top and a circular pea-stone drive leading to the columned front door.

Capturing all the Vineyard's romance and nostalgia on the outside, the house is thoroughly modern within, the traditional finishes notwithstanding. The open and light-filled spaces flow, one to the other, inviting you inside and then back out onto the terraces, a circulation pattern that allows the home to live bigger than its square footage would suggest. The design is endlessly expandable and entirely adaptable, as easily cloaked in southwestern stucco or California Craftsman style as in this Vineyard look.

ABOVE: The entry foyer leads directly into the great room, providing the house with a generous sense of space, even though the overall scale of the home is quite intimate.

OPPOSITE: The kitchen opens directly from the great room, allowing for easy flow and increasing accessibility when the homeowners entertain.

ABOVE, TOP AND BOTTOM: With its tufted settee and French doors leading to a private courtyard, the master bathroom proves a wonderful place to relax.

RIGHT: Beautifully framed multipaned windows, including those in the clerestory and the French doors, convey the unequivocally New England character of the master bedroom, while the antique-beamed ceiling continues the rustic theme of the former fishing shack first established in the great room.

FOLLOWING PAGES: The home's right and left wings, connected to the central structure by Chippendale-railing-topped glazed breezeways, enclose and embrace a bluestone rear terrace outfitted with grilling, dining, and gathering areas, as well as an outdoor shower. This space seamlessly transitions to the yard, where a cupola-topped dog house shares its aesthetic with that of the rest of the property.

6

On The Water

Like all our projects, the seaside homes we create for clients celebrate both the rich vintage design vernaculars of their locations and the joys of contemporary living. But these properties must also pay particular attention to the uniqueness of their waterfront sites. Whether historic structures or historically motivated new-builds, these residences make the most of their settings. They take maximum advantage of water views, clear daylight, and sea air, while at the same time remaining highly sensitive to their often-fragile position where the land meets the ocean.

This translates most obviously into a use of poetic architectural elements that increase the beauty of a home and simultaneously bring the outdoors in and the indoors out. Broad expanses of windows and glass doors — plus generous decks, patios, and covered porches — capitalize on ample cross breezes, warmth from the sun, and long vistas. They all have the benefit of making a home more attractive when seen from afar, too.

Building by the water involves other, less romantic, considerations as well — ones that can significantly influence programmatic and aesthetic aspects of a home's design. These include height restrictions and setbacks mandated by zoning and conservation commissions and the need to withstand strong winds and driving rain, floods, and erosion.

I've discovered that the constraints of coastal development produce as many opportunities for creative design solutions as they do complications. The responses I've developed have proved capable of not only meeting the challenges of waterfront design but becoming aesthetic assets.

When it comes to seaside zoning and environmental regulations, I've found ways to meet height restrictions and setback requirements without sacrificing the size of a home or the appeal of its coastal location. By subtly setting the structure into the ground or placing floor joists into a foundation rather than on top of it — or even by re-landscaping to lower an entire property below its original grade — we're able to build two or even three stories where others may have fit only one. And we do so without causing a house to look oversized.

Should basements be disallowed by a high water table or FEMA regulations, I move the recreational and service spaces to a multipurpose ground floor, a strategy that has the supplemental benefit of lifting all the most-used more-formal public spaces to a second level, improving their sea views.

To protect against the ravages of wind, rain, and other weather, I add layers of retaining walls, porches, decks, and terraces that provide a first line of defense against storms coming off the sea. These, of course, create the exact sort of indoor/outdoor living spaces contemporary clients crave. And because the aesthetic of these elements accords with that of traditional New England waterfront residences, they assist in making a home's historic narrative ring true.

When working on the coast, I frequently design long, narrow houses to better exploit the views and light. The risk is that the resulting structures look out of scale. Layers of weather-mitigating indoor-outdoor spaces — together with variations in the depth of façade details and attention to the solid-void relationship between windows and walls — help break up the mass of these larger buildings.

As the houses in the following pages make clear, we don't just want coastal residences to appear timeless. We want them to withstand the test of time — and all the buffeting of sun, salt air, and stormy weather that entails.

ABOVE, TOP: When designing coastal homes, I find it as important to consider how the house is viewed from the water as it is to think about the water views themselves. Acting like something of a lighthouse, this shingle-style pool cabana in Edgartown, for example, serves as a glowing beacon visible from both land and sea.

ABOVE, BOTTOM: To meet FEMA regulations, the first floor of this Edgartown boathouse serves as storage while the second floor hosts an entertaining space with panoramic views of the lively harbor.

OPPOSITE: A pergola outside this Edgartown pool cabana provides partial shade to a casual dining area, smoothing the transition from the building's interiors to the sun-bathed pool terrace, fire pit seating area, and water views.

OPPOSITE, TOP AND BOTTOM: In Vineyard Haven, on Martha's Vineyard, I expanded an existing 1950s house in order to keep the home as close to the water as possible. Grandfathered into less-restrictive setback regulations, the original structure now serves as a stone-and-brick base that anchors the new sections to a shorefront rock outcropping.

ABOVE: The highly animated interior living areas of this re-imagined captain's house open directly to outdoor terraces, a pool, and the edge of Edgartown Harbor. One of the most treasured spaces is the spar-varnished mahogany bar in the restored boathouse.

SOUTH SHORE SLEIGHT OF HAND

Cohassett, Massachusetts

Transforming this waterside property from the two-story mid-century-modern kit house it once was into a gambrel-roofed four-and-a-half-story shingle-style home was no small task. It required more than a bit of smoke and mirrors, not to mention innovation and ingenuity; in-depth understanding of the tight, wooded lot's inclined topography; and a firm grasp of the zoning and conservation rules governing it.

RIGHT: To transform a small 1950s harbor-side deck house in Cohasset, on Massachusetts's South Shore, into a significantly larger gambrel-style home, I re-graded the challenging, sloped property. This allowed me to keep the size of the new front façade in scale with its surroundings, while expanding the square footage and opening the back to the water.

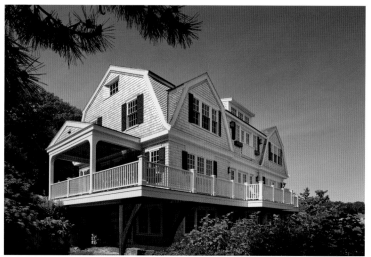

ABOVE, LEFT: The screened porch provides an indoor-outdoor oasis for people to gather and enjoy views of the gardens and Little Harbor, while keeping warm by the fireplace.

ABOVE, RIGHT: Conservation Commission guidelines prevented the footprint of the house from expanding. I found a solution to this challenge — and created a signature aesthetic element — by designing a cantilevered wraparound deck supported by dramatic flying buttresses.

OPPOSITE: All but undetectable from the front, the home's four-story rear harbor-side elevation truly expresses the magic of the site, taking full advantage of the property's grade change, forested setting, and harbor frontage.

When the clients commissioned us, we found the original structure — which sits on an inlet of Little Harbor, in the town of Cohasset, on Massachusetts's South Shore — in disarray. Sunk into a rocky, humid harbor-side hollow, it had become a moldy mess after suffering through decades of exposure to moisture and weather. We didn't want to tear it down, however, because current regulations disallowed rebuilding as close to the shore. Instead, we needed to preserve what we could, then vertically expand the building to meet the clients' large program, finishing it both inside and out to capture the charm of New England's vernacular coastal architecture. We did all this while keeping the front façade modest and letting the back take full advantage of the steeply sloped terrain and east-facing water views.

Our novel solution was to essentially bury the original house, adjusting the property's topography to turn the first floor into a largely subterranean level and then building anew both on top of and below it. This preserved the original footprint — a zoning requirement — but allowed expansion up and down and, through smart cantilevering, side to side.

Today, as you approach the home from the front, it appears as a twenty-six-foot-tall cottage. But its water-facing rear elevation reveals its hidden breadth. The four and a half floors of windows and French doors, plus a cantilevered wraparound deck, screened porch, dormers, and elevated balconies offer uninterrupted water views and make a sophisticated statement to anyone admiring the property from across the harbor — one in keeping with Cohasset's quintessential small-town New England aesthetic. Though the house is now quite expansive, these elements serve to break down the mass of the back façade and keep it feeling entirely in scale with its surroundings. Nestled into the hollow's trees and rocky cliffs, the almost entirely new home looks as if it had always been part of the natural landscape.

OPPOSITE: Natural light floods into the spacious two-story foyer from clerestory windows.

RIGHT: A new, open stairway — featuring historically accurate, intricately turned balustrades and newel posts — links the home's several stories both visually and practically.

FOLLOWING PAGES: Overlooking the harbor and ocean, the open-plan living room, dining room, and kitchen are filled with suggestions of a bygone era. Antique beams, for example, extend down from the ceiling to form a mantel over the home's original Rumford fireplace.

LEFT AND ABOVE: Not only do the living and dining areas graciously flow from one room to the next, they also lead seamlessly to the cantilevered deck and the outdoors through multiple sets of French doors. The kitchen, which centers on an island outfitted with open wine display and storage, becomes an extension of these gathering and entertaining spaces.

OPPOSITE: The porch, with its white-painted brick fireplace, beamed ceilings, and all but invisible screen walls, feels like it's part of both the home's interior and the great outdoors.

ABOVE: The master suite's built-in headboard dresser anchors the floating bed in the middle of the room. It also allows the space to remain largely free of furniture — ensuring that nothing distracts from its sweeping, top-floor views.

FOLLOWING PAGES: Thanks to another clerestory window, as well as a set of French doors opening to a Romeo and Juliet balcony, the study, which is also set in the home's highest story, revels in a tremendous amount of morning light and seemingly endless views over Little Harbor and the Atlantic.

DOWNSTAIRS, UPSTAIRS

Edgartown, Martha's Vineyard, Massachusetts

SET ON AN OCEAN-SIDE street on Martha's Vineyard, this double-gabled residence is what's known as an upside-down house. Because the property is separated from the sea by the drive and high sand dunes beyond, only those rooms on its upper floor enjoy water views. The clients wanted to capture as much of the vista from as many primary rooms as possible, however.

RIGHT: Maximizing the water views from this new-build family compound in Edgartown required quite a bit of ingenuity. Its position across the street from the Atlantic and behind high dunes meant that I had to place the main house's primary living areas upstairs but still keep the spaces on the ground floor lively and engaging.

RIGHT: I activated the ground floor by connecting it directly to the property's vibrant alfresco living room: an Olympic-size pool flanked by the pergolas of a cabana and an outdoor kitchen. The bay on the right side of the rear façade hides a staircase that connects the pool and yard to the living spaces above.

FOLLOWING PAGES: A two-way fireplace in the outdoor kitchen offers a link between the pool and the bocce court.

As a result, although a typical residence would have such major public spaces as the kitchen and dining, family, and living areas on its ground floor, all of these, as well as the master suite, needed to be on the second level of this house. A scheme like this, which homeowners frequently request when building on the water, poses its share of difficulties. Figuring out how to make the viewless ground floor not just functional but desirable is a challenge, as is determining how to best handle vertical circulation to and from the second level, both inside and out.

To enliven the ground floor, I kept it clearly connected to the property's abundant opportunities for outdoor activity. From the front door, you can see all the way through the foyer and family room to French doors that lead to a covered porch and Olympic-size pool. Not only does this open plan let in plenty of light, but it pulls you through the house to the enticements of the yard, which, beyond the pool, include an outdoor kitchen, fireplace, pergola, and dining area, plus vegetable garden, bocce court, and cabana.

Upstairs, the house is essentially one-room deep, so every space — from kitchen to dining area, great room to master suite — has superlative water views and access to the second-floor deck. To seamlessly connect this level to the pool and yard, I devised a pair of two-story bays that push out from the rear façade, bookending the deck and covered porch below. The bay on the west side encloses a ground-floor screened porch that's especially enjoyable at sunset, while the one opposite solves the circulation challenge with a hidden staircase that connects the house from top to bottom, allowing easy access to the pool and yard from the second floor, and vice versa.

ABOVE: Because the home's main entrance is on the ground floor and the primary living space is above, I designed a particularly inviting and delicately conceived stairway system (RIGHT) that would immediately draw residents and guests upstairs.

OPPOSITE: To give the homeowners and their guests further reason to spend time on the ground floor, I designed a fun and welcoming bar area and kitchenette. It provides direct access to a screened porch through a foldaway wall of glass doors.

FOLLOWING PAGES: The top-floor great room's broad expanse of windows celebrates the water views, while the articulated trim and antique wooden beams framing the beadboard ceiling add layers of texture and depth to the design scheme.

ABOVE: A set of pocket doors in the dining room conceal a small private office. The transom above lets natural light penetrate into what would otherwise be a dark space.

RIGHT: The richly trimmed ceiling treatment carries into the dining room from the great room. This creates the illusion that the two rooms comprise one continuous space, even though they are connected only by two deep portals.

FOLLOWING PAGES: The gray stain on the richly grained kitchen cabinets recalls the color, tone, and texture of the driftwood that washes ashore on the coast of New England.

ABOVE: A similar but simplified ceiling treatment extends into the master bedroom. Its antique beams and beadboard reinforce the home's historic character, while its relative lack of embellishment helps establish the room's calm atmosphere.

OPPOSITE: I found inspiration for the master suite's formal, wood-paneled dressing room in the interiors of opulent ocean liners of the early 1900s.

RIGHT: The crisp, clean lines of the master bathroom offer a modernist counterpoint to the space's more traditional walnut finishes and honed Carrera marble countertops.

FOLLOWING PAGES: At dusk, the windowed rear façade glows from within, and a fire burns in the outdoor kitchen, welcoming guests for quiet evenings or more raucous revels.

ENTERTAINING BY THE SEA

Edgartown Harbor, Martha's Vineyard, Massachusetts

THIS HOME, PERCHED ATOP A KNOLL in Edgartown, on Martha's Vineyard, has everything people love about coastal New England architecture. The picturesque widow's walk, second-floor decks, and walls of multipaned windows and glass doors provide phenomenal harbor vistas, and the dramatic oversailing eaves in the four gambrels reinforce the historically motivated design of the shingle-style new-build construction.

RIGHT: Hidden from the public road, this Edgartown home is accessed by a long, curving cobblestone driveway. This creates a tremendous sense of anticipation, ultimately revealing the large, double-gambrel house in all its grandeur, while concealing its water views until one enters the foyer.

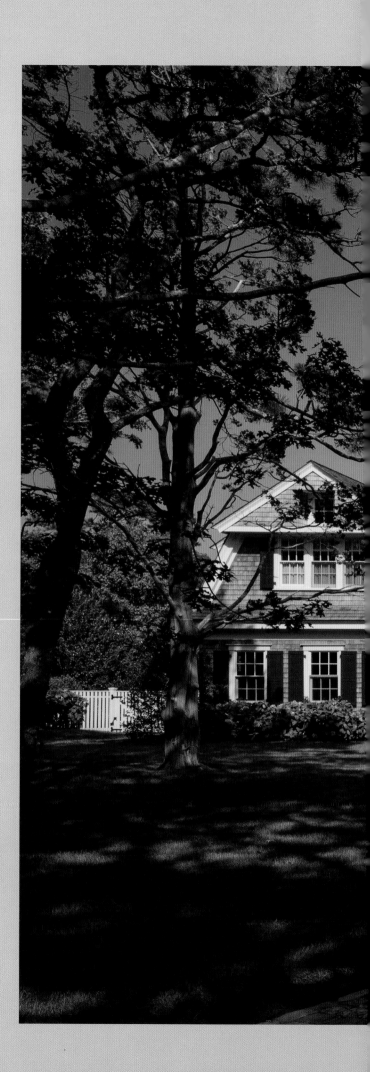

LEFT: The guest suite sits above the carriage house wing, removing it from the rest of the house and assuring its privacy.

OPPOSITE: Simultaneously maximizing the livable square footage on the upper floor and allowing the home to feel shorter than it actually is, the gambrel roof creates a historically correct sense of scale. This feeling of appropriateness extends to the detailing and proportions of the façade's fixtures and trim.

FOLLOWING PAGES: The floor plan's formal spine — off of which the home's primary spaces unfold — begins in the wainscoted foyer.

Inside, high ceilings create an expansive feeling, rich classical detailing instills a sense of nostalgia, and enfilades of rooms set along two primary spines make for long views through the home and out to the sea and gardens. Perhaps best of all, these spines resolve themselves in three different covered outdoor living areas offering abundant space for alfresco entertaining — a key component of the clients' large program.

And large it was, ultimately comprising 14,000 square feet in a main house, carriage house wing, guesthouse, and gatehouse, including great room, library, seven bedrooms, and even a bowling alley. All this had to be contained within a height of just twenty-six feet, as required by waterfront zoning regulations, and at a significant setback from the sea, as stipulated by the conservation commission. The neighborhood association also demanded that homes remain invisible from the road. The gambrel roof provided the perfect solution, enabling the greatest ceiling heights and usable upper-level square footage to be held within a vernacular type that appears smaller than it is. Since the clients wanted a wide swath of uninterrupted outdoor space for garden parties, the setback stipulation turned into an advantage, too.

We oriented the home to face east, the better to catch the fantastic morning light that streams in over the water, especially in the second-floor master bedroom and study. The pool sits to the south, enjoying even more sun and keeping the backyard open for entertaining. The three covered porches — including one connecting the main house with the guesthouse, which includes an outdoor fireplace — similarly enjoy the best eastward water views and light and simultaneously protect the buildings from the elements.

ABOVE: The spine extends from the foyer through a cased archway to the living room, granting long views through the house from the moment one enters.

OPPOSITE: The breakfast room, finished with beadboard-covered walls, antique flooring, and a built-in banquette, enjoys views of the pool from a windowed alcove.

FOLLOWING PAGES: Extensive glazing allows the walls of the large kitchen to all but disappear, making the space feel like it's part of the pool terrace, back yard, and harbor beyond.

ABOVE: From the entry, the primary spine also extends through three enfiladed spaces, culminating at a framed view of the stone fireplace on one of the home's two covered porches.

RIGHT: I used salvaged antique wood flooring to panel the library, adding a warm element to the house.

FOLLOWING PAGES: Designed for waterfront entertaining, this covered porch on the harbor-facing side of the house opens off a party room whose folding wall of glass doors erases any separation between indoors and out.

PATRICK AHEARN

ABOVE: With its series of screened and covered porches, open terraces and decks on both its first and second floors, the home's seaside façade celebrates the best of summer on the coast of New England.

ABOVE AND OPPOSITE: Located to one side of
the house, the pool terrace becomes an outdoor
room of its own, with separate spaces for dining
and lounging. The pool cabana doubles as an
indoor-outdoor entertaining space, with a pergola
for sunny days and a fireplace for cool evenings.

FOLLOWING PAGES: The symmetry of the
primary façade — with its widow's walk flanked
by exaggerated stone chimneys and its entry
portal framed by manicured boxwoods fronted
by a broad cobblestone motor court — honors the
romance and history of New England's vernacular
architecture in the most timeless and welcoming
of ways.

AFTERWORD

I've devoted the most recent decades of my career to creating timeless homes that blend the best of past and present. But the time I spent earlier working on adaptive-reuse urban design and commercial projects instilled in me an appreciation for the central values that have informed all the residences I've done since.

My application of the greater-good theory to architecture grew directly out of the respect for scale and density and the sensitivity to history and context that I developed while designing those large-scale projects in places as far-flung as the Middle East and as close to home as Boston and Martha's Vineyard. They required me to develop strategies and skills for making not just spaces but *places*: active and engaging destinations that would improve communities and enhance lives.

All these commissions centered on the seamless combination of old and new, necessitating an appreciation of the importance of centuries-old structures and a knowledge of local vernacular styles. This led me to carefully study the elements that give an existing building or town square — or even an entire village or city — its unique character. My goals were always the same: to preserve the unique qualities of what had come before, enhance what already existed, and imagine what might have been. I did all that while adding new value and contemporary appeal that would make a historic place relevant and give it meaning for decades to come.

Establishing a script for a project proved one of the most effective ways to remake historic buildings. My work on the reimagining of Boston's disused Faneuil Hall as an active urban marketplace with cultural, retail, and culinary offerings while part of Benjamin Thompson Associates showed me how to spin a story that would weave together past and present. Our presentations to developers and city stakeholders involved elaborate slideshows with multimedia elements. We captivated audiences with images of kids on bikes, flower vendors, and food stalls, atmospheric music and aspirational ideas.

The value of the narrative concept we presented was borne out by the tremendous success of the final product. These days, eighteen million people pass through Faneuil Hall's various spaces each year, making it one of the seven most-visited attractions in the world. And in 2009, the American Institute of Architects bestowed its Twenty-Five Year Award on the project, celebrating the longevity of the accomplishment.

We also applied similar scripting strategies to festival marketplace and waterfront revival projects in Miami and Baltimore, as well as to new-build, mixed-use hotels and urban design initiatives in Cairo and Abu Dhabi. These narratives brought a piece of architecture to life, just like the scripts I spin today for residential clients.

Commercial work crystallized my thinking in particular about the importance of the space between and around buildings, which led to my creation of campus-like configurations for residential properties. A public plaza between structures in projects like Faneuil Hall Marketplace becomes a private courtyard flanked by historic farmhouse and a newly built pool cabana in a Martha's Vineyard property.

The value I came to place on alfresco living areas like these, as well as easy connections between indoors and out, goes hand in hand with the attention I learned to pay to the space between buildings. The garage-style doors on the sides of Faneuil Hall, for example, which are raised in the warmer months, all but erase any barrier between the marketplace's interior and the adjacent open-air plazas.

For my later revitalization of the Newbury Street commercial corridor in Boston's Back Bay, I designed restaurants and storefronts whose windowed walls open up, connecting a café or boutique to the scene outside and the larger urban environment beyond. Tables spilled onto the sidewalk from eateries, as did displays of clothing and other merchandise from shops. This encouraged passersby to weave in and out, grabbing a bite or browsing as they walked down the newly enlivened street. I brought a similar thought process, and applied the same urban design

OPPOSITE: Over the course of my more than forty years as a practicing architect, I've completed over four hundred projects in one of Boston's most historic neighborhoods, the Back Bay.

ABOVE: While working in the 1970s as a young architect at Benjamin Thompson Associates, in Cambridge, Massachusetts, I had the privilege to contribute to the reinvention of Boston's centuries-old Faneuil Hall. We transformed the building from a disused shell into a festival marketplace and public urban space that combines history with contemporary culinary, retail, and entertainment attractions.

PATRICK AHEARN

OPPOSITE: My work in Boston historic neighborhoods extends from the Back Bay's Newbury Street (TOP, LEFT AND RIGHT), where I enlivened the retail corridor with open-air street-front cafes, to Beacon Hill (BOTTOM, RIGHT), where I sensitively preserved landmarked façades and designed modern interiors within, to the South End (BOTTOM, LEFT), where I created new garden-level courtyard apartments with private entrances below front stoops.

RIGHT: The development and design of Edgartown's Atlantic restaurant and Boathouse club — which replaced a nondescript mid-twentieth-century building — served as catalysts for the revitalization of the village's downtown waterfront.

lessons of historic preservation and contemporary innovation, to the renovation of famed classic hotels up and down the East Coast, from Boston's Fairmont Copley Plaza and Omni Parker House to the Shoreham in Washington, D.C., and South Florida's Boca Raton Hotel. At each, I looked for ways not only to restore architectural elements but also to relaunch these properties as preeminent social, cultural, culinary, and entertainment destinations within their cities.

To that end, I reimagined underused lobbies and mezzanines, turning them into restaurants and cafés that often connect indoors and out, and I took back offices with underutilized views of gardens or courtyards and reclaimed them as public-facing spaces. I even made the most of basements. At Presidente InterContinental Mexico City (then known as El Presidente) for example, we broke open the street-level floor plate to flood a subterranean space with sun from above and installed a wall of windows on one end that looked into a newly excavated walled courtyard. Thanks to this intervention, the former basement became a lively, light-filled restaurant, filled with guests and locals every night of the week.

Back in Boston, my work extended well past Newbury Street and Faneuil Hall deep into the city's most beloved neighborhoods, where I restored and reimagined hundreds of townhouses, most from the nineteenth century. When I first came to Boston, in 1973, many of the grand buildings of the Back Bay, Beacon Hill, and the South End had been abandoned, boarded up, and left to deteriorate. I saw the value and, just as important, the potential in these structures, and I devoted the early years of my solo practice almost exclusively to their renaissance. This work led to a prolonged period of condominium conversions in Boston that gave the city's historic districts a second life. Over the course of thirty years, I renovated some four hundred buildings there.

I once again applied lessons from Faneuil Hall Marketplace and Newbury Street, this time to private domestic dwellings, painstakingly preserving the landmark-protected façades of these homes. In the Back Bay, I opened up the townhouses' floor plans to allow for easy flow and circulation, and I turned formerly unusable attics into mansard-roofed or dormered penthouses. I added double-height windows and glass doors to the Charles River–facing side of row houses whose rear elevations weren't landmarked. I created gardens on roofs, as well as balconies and terraces on top of back-alley garages, which I sometimes converted to artist studios or guest quarters. I activated those all-important spaces between buildings to re-energize a dormant district.

In the South End, I was often able to carve out two levels of garden apartments that enjoyed private under-stoop entries and plenty of natural light from enclosed courtyards to their rear. On Beacon Hill, I restored and preserved the original primary façades, while enhancing hidden gardens with indoor/outdoor living spaces. All these were innovations, brand new to Boston and elsewhere.

Commercial developers came to love how my creative solutions maximized the square footage of their salable space; prospective homeowners loved how my renovations restored a sense of romance and nostalgia that had been missing from these neighborhoods for years, while letting them live the way they wanted; and landmark preservation commissions loved that I accomplished all this without compromising the historic fabric of a neighborhood — in fact, these projects enhanced it.

After buying our first home in Edgartown, on Martha's Vineyard, in the late 1980s, I began thinking about leveraging the lessons of my past work to rejuvenate and reenergize the historic village's small harbor-side downtown. This core area had developed in a somewhat haphazard manner, starting as early as the late 1600s. Very little had been done, however, to ensure that more recent aesthetic choices were in line with the look and feel of the past.

LEFT AND OPPOSITE: Widening the brick sidewalk outside of the Boathouse and Atlantic and adding outdoor dining animated Edgartown's lower Main Street (LEFT). The pathways around the club and restaurant now encourage public access to the harbor (OPPOSITE), which further enhances the building's contribution to the greater good of the community.

FOLLOWING PAGES: Classically New England in character — with its weathered-shingle exterior and six-over-one windows — the Boathouse and Atlantic feel equally timeless inside. The club, for example, takes its aesthetic cues from the traditional nautical finishes and details of the sailboats and yachts that have plied the waters around Cape Cod and the Islands for decades.

Over the years, aluminum siding, asphalt roof tiles, fluorescent lighting, and windows with plastic frames, smoked-glass panes, and snap-in mullions had come to mar the centuries-old commercial streetscapes. But it wasn't just the aesthetic that failed to live up to Edgartown's potential. The downtown program also fell well short of the needs and expectations of an increasingly affluent, youthful, and discriminating clientele, including owners of vacation homes who were spending more and more time on the island. Main Street had T-shirt stores and tourist-oriented inexpensive gift shops aplenty, but good restaurants, quality fashion and design boutiques, and art galleries were few and far between.

I decided to present a proposal to the Edgartown Board of Trade for the revitalization of this dense and highly walkable commercial district. Something between a visual primer and a master plan, it laid out a series of ideas to restore to the village the character and charm bestowed by its long history and waterfront location. There would be changes large and small, from entirely new storefronts to brick sidewalks instead of concrete, flowers in wooden planters, vintage-inspired street lighting, clear plate-glass windows, wooden doors, and improved signage to welcome and entice prospective customers.

The plan was never realized, but as longtime residents, retailers, restaurateurs, and real estate owners saw the smart and sensitive residential projects I was doing around town, they came to me, and together we began making enhancements.

Perhaps the greatest catalyst for this was the Atlantic and Boathouse, which I cofounded and whose building, on the harbor at the very end of Main Street, I designed. We turned a dilapidated 1960s eyesore known as the Navigator Building into a shingle-style structure with an appropriately nautical look and feel. Upstairs, it now houses the convivial spaces of the private Boathouse club and, on the street level, the dining room, covered porches, and sidewalk seating of the bustling Atlantic restaurant. For the public at large, we added wide brick walkways and outdoor furniture on the Main Street side, as well as access to and broad views of the waterfront — none of which existed before our intervention.

Bit by bit, the atmosphere of Edgartown started to improve — proving that small changes slowly rendered can make the greater-good theory a reality.

I continue to play an active role in the ongoing restoration and remerchandising of Edgartown's downtown, which, thanks to projects like the Atlantic and Boathouse, has reclaimed the look and feel of a classical New England seaport, albeit one with amenities selected and designed to serve a twenty-first-century audience.

Today, when I drive around the village or walk through its downtown core, I see an ensemble of more than 160 buildings and other spaces my firm has made or restored. Collectively, the urban design and commercial commissions I've completed in Edgartown over the past twenty-five-plus years — in addition to the scores of houses I've worked on there — constitute the greatest project of my career, the one of which I am most proud. More than four decades into my time as an architect, these place-making ventures continue to keep me excited and intrigued, and more enthusiastic than ever about my craft.

PATRICK AHEARN

ACKNOWLEDGEMENTS

This book has given me the opportunity to reflect on over forty-three years of practice, thirty-nine of which have been with my own firm. Throughout these years, I have grown and continue to grow as an architect. The experiences and the people that I have engaged with during the course of my career are near and dear to me. The multiple and mutual friendships that were formed in the process of creating these wonderful homes have enriched my life in so many ways.

Designing a home for an individual or family is a very personal and reflective process for both the client and the architect. The design process affords all parties an opportunity to explore not only how one wants to live, but also to better understand the true meaning of "hearth and home." My work, whether it's new construction, historic restoration, or renovation, is rooted in the notion that historical context, either reimagined or based on fact, creates the foundation for "timeless" architecture. My houses are not museums, but homes that function and flow in a manner that reflects how people live today.

The eighteen homes illustrated and the accompanying narrative in the book provide a glimpse into my design process that culminates with these richly detailed homes. Each celebrates my application of the greater-good theory to architecture and is rooted in a keen sense of place. One of my mantras is "it's all about scale," which includes the scale of individual buildings as well as their scalability in the context of the surrounding locale.

These goals and objectives are shared by everyone in my firm. The majority of my team has been with me for many years, as we collectively see with the same set of eyes and believe in the same approach to creating timeless architecture. These incredibly talented and insightful people include Michael Tartamella AIA, Cesar Monte, Jim Golden AIA, Michael Cahn, Peter Fletcher, Colby Mauke, Eddie Gaffney, Katie Nolan, Karen Beck, and of course, my loyal sister, Nancy Ahearn.

I've also had the great opportunity to work with many skilled builders, each one bringing a keen understanding of local construction methods and techniques that continue to enhance our work with authenticity and genuineness. They include Bryan Sweeney, Jack Sullivan, Peter Fallon, Jon Wardwell, Norman Rankow, Peter Rosbeck, Gerret Conover, Adam Moran, E.J. Jaxtimer, Doug Whitla, Steve Fabrizio, Elias Constantopoulos, and Steve Colclough to name a few.

While the builders bring our designs to fruition, the landscape designers seamlessly blend the homes with the natural environment as the interior designers bring our homes to life. I would like to thank Donaroma's Nursery & Landscape Services, Dan Gordon, Mike Coutu, Cate Caruso, John Murphy, Jim Gauthier, Susan Stacy, and Andrea Georgopolis among many others.

I also want to thank the many terrific magazine editors who have supported my work over the years and the creative photographers, Greg Premru and Michael Partenio, who have brought my work to the public realm so beautifully. I am forever grateful.

My life has also been enriched by the wonderful collaborations I have had prior to forming my own practice from my days at Benjamin Thompson Associates and The Architects Collaborative. These talented colleagues have had a lasting impression and inspiration on my work. They include Ben Thompson, Bruno D'Agostino, Rick Lamb, Sam Fan, Keith Patterson, John Sheehy, Bill Pressley, Mike Gebhart, Morse Payne, and of course, my mentor to whom this book is dedicated, Howard Elkus.

I also must thank my clients, not only for the opportunity to partner with them on the design of their homes, but also for their friendship, trust, and confidence over all these years. It is truly a gift.

In creating this book, it took many hands to guide me through the process. I want to thank Gordon Goff at ORO Editions for his interest in publishing the book and his guidance in its creation along with managing editor, Jake Anderson, and book designer, Pablo Mandel. I must thank Jill Cohen for her directness and fortitude when reviewing and appropriately editing our work to tell my story so succinctly and my writer, Andrew Sessa, for the hours spent listening to my life story and assisting me with creating the narrative for this book. I must also thank everyone involved in marketing the book including my dear friend (and client), Josh McCall, for his invaluable insight and Rebecca Booma. This truly was a memorable experience.

Finally, I must thank my wife, Marsha, my most sensitive critic, for her keen sense of appropriateness and her support over the last thirty years.

PROJECT CREDITS

A Blacksmith's Home Reborn
BUILDER: Colonial Reproductions, Inc.
INTERIOR DESIGNER: Paula Conover
LANDSCAPE: Donaroma's Nursery & Landscape Services

Whaling's Golden Era
BUILDER: Rosbeck Builders Corporation
INTERIOR DESIGNER: Rooms & Gardens
LANDSCAPE: Donaroma's Nursery & Landscape Services

Correcting the Historical Record
BUILDER: Colonial Reproductions, Inc.
INTERIOR DESIGNER: Tracker Home Decor
LANDSCAPE: Donaroma's Nursery & Landscape Services

A Cottage with Room to Grow
BUILDER: Fallon Custom Homes & Renovations and Sweeney Custom Homes & Renovations
INTERIOR DESIGNER: Marsha Ahearn
LANDSCAPE: Angelo Santucci, Inc.

Royal Barry Wills Reconsidered
BUILDER: Sweeney Custom Homes & Renovations
LANDSCAPE: Sudbury Design Group, Inc.

The Jewel in the Chatham Crown
BUILDER: Whitla Brothers Builders, Inc.
INTERIOR DESIGNER: Homeowner
LANDSCAPE: Patrick Ahearn Architect LLC

Reviving a Greek Revival
BUILDER: Colonial Reproductions, Inc.
INTERIOR DESIGNER: Homeowner
LANDSCAPE: Peggy Schwier Gardens

A Cottage by the Sea
BUILDER: Conover Restorations, Inc.
INTERIOR DESIGNER: STUDIO C
LANDSCAPE: Donaroma's Nursery & Landscape Services

From Darkness to Light
BUILDER: E. J. Jaxtimer Builder, Inc.
INTERIOR DESIGNER: Anthony Catalfano Interiors
LANDSCAPE: Phyllis W. Cole Landscapes

Inventing Character on Martha's Vineyard
BUILDER: Colonial Reproductions, Inc.
INTERIOR DESIGNER: Marsha Ahearn
LANDSCAPE: Donaroma's Nursery & Landscape Services

A Greek Revival Retreat for a Blended Family
BUILDER: Hob Knob Construction
INTERIOR DESIGNER: Tracker Home Decor
LANDSCAPE: Donaroma's Nursery & Landscape Services

Weathering the Storm
BUILDER: Colonial Reproductions, Inc.
INTERIOR DESIGNER: Cynthia Thomas Interiors
LANDSCAPE: Donaroma's Nursery & Landscape Services

An Opulent Take on Turn-of-the-Century Style
BUILDER: Stonehedge Developments
INTERIOR DESIGNER: Kate Coughlin Interiors
LANDSCAPE: Robert Ferre Landscaping

A Vineyard Home Puts its Best Façade Forward
BUILDER: Rosbeck Builders Corporation
INTERIOR DESIGNER: Gauthier-Stacy, Inc.
LANDSCAPE: Donaroma's Nursery & Landscape Services

Made for TV
BUILDER: Timothy McHugh Builders, Inc.
INTERIOR DESIGNER: Linda Woodrum
LANDSCAPE: Donaroma's Nursery & Landscape Services

South Shore Sleight of Hand
BUILDER: Colclough Construction
INTERIOR DESIGNER: Homeowner
LANDSCAPE: Paragon Landscape Design, Inc.

Downstairs, Upstairs
BUILDER: Rosbeck Builders Corporation
INTERIOR DESIGNER: Slifer Designs
LANDSCAPE: Dan Gordon Landscape Architects

Entertaining by the Sea
BUILDER: Colonial Reproductions, Inc.
INTERIOR DESIGNER: Gauthier-Stacy, Inc.
LANDSCAPE: Donaroma's Nursery & Landscape Services

PHOTOGRAPHY
AND BOOK CREDITS

Patrick Ahearn: page 63 (left)

Phillip Ahearn: pages 14–15

Taylor Ahearn: pages 238 (top left)

Randi Baird Photography: jacket headshot

© Can Stock Photo Inc. / marcorubino: page 306

Steve Dunwell Photography: pages 307, 308 (top left, bottom left, bottom right)

Sam Gray: pages 224–25

Gil Jacobs Photography: page 200 (top)

Keller & Keller. Reprinted with permission from *Decorating Magazine*. © 2007 Meredith Corporation. All rights reserved: pages 62, 63 (right), 64–67

Levittown Public Library: page 16

Richard Mandelkorn Photography: pages 6, 19 (bottom), 20 (top left), 59

Martha's Vineyard Museum: pages 30, 33 (bottom)

Katherine Nolan: page 308 (top right)

Patrick Ahearn Architect LLC: pages 18, 167 (left)

Michael Partenio: pages 108–09, 111, 113, 119, 121 (right), 124 (top left), 125, 167 (right), 170–77, 250, 266–67, 270–71, 280–81

    Reprinted with permission from *Beautiful Homes Magazine*. © 2006 Meredith Corporation. All rights reserved: pages 180–87, 189–93

    Reprinted with permission from *Beautiful Homes Magazine*. © 2009 Meredith Corporation. All rights reserved: pages 94–95, 149 (top left), 202 (right)

    Reprinted with permission from *Beautiful Homes Magazine*. © 2009 Meredith Corporation. All rights reserved: pages 150–57, 160

Kent Pell: pages 70–71, 200 (bottom)

Greg Premru Photography: jacket, end sheets, pages 2–3, 9–13, 19 (top), 20 (top right, bottom left, bottom right), 21 (top left, top right, bottom left), 23–25, 26 (bottom), 27–29, 31–32, 33 (top), 34–58, 60–61, 68–69, 72–93, 96–107, 110, 112, 114–17, 120, 121 (top left, bottom left), 122–23, 124 (bottom left), 126–27, 145–48, 149 (top right, bottom left), 158–59, 161–66, 168–69, 178–79, 188, 194–99, 201, 202 (left), 203–23, 226–37, 239–49, 251–65, 268–69, 272–79, 282–305, 309–16

Eric Roth Photography: pages 21 (bottom right), 128–43

Douglas P. Whitla: page 26 (top)

TEXT BY Patrick Ahearn

WRITTEN WITH Andrew Sessa

P.A. ARCHITECT MARKETING DIRECTOR Katherine Nolan

ORO EDITIONS MANAGING EDITOR Jake Anderson

BOOK DESIGNER Pablo Mandel / CircularStudio.com